Hi

Thank you for
your kind support!

ENJOY THIS
AMAZING DAY!

1. faul

Psalm 27:3

DARE TO LIVE GREATLY

Real Christian Living Requires the Grit, Courage & Confidence of a Navy SEAL in Training

L. C. Fowler
Basic Underwater Demolition SEAL (BUD/S) Class 89

Join the NavySeal.com conversation and
receive newsletters, free offers & invitations.
Go to NavySeal.com
NavySeal.com is not a government agency.

2020 Gold Award, Nonfiction Authors Association / National Indie Excellence Awards Finalist / B.R.A.G Medallion Honoree/ New York City Book Award 2021 Gold Medal Winner

Join the NavySeal.com conversation and receive newsletters, free offers & invitations. Go to NavySeal.com

NavySeal.com is not a government agency.

(For copyright information, ISBN, and other editions, please see Publication Details.)

———————————

Dare to Live Greatly: Real Christian Living Requires the Grit,
Courage & Confidence of a Navy SEAL in Training (Formerly *Dare to Live Greatly:*
The Courage to Live a Powerful Christian Life)
© 2019, 2021 by Larry Fowler.

ISBNs: 978-1-7339880-6-3 (hc);
978-1-7339880-4-9 (pbk);
978-1-7339880-5-6 (ebk)

Go to NavySeal.com for stories about or written by famed members of the Navy Special Warfare community.

Italics in Scripture quotations are the author's emphasis. Scripture quotations are from:

The Holy Bible, New Living Translation (nlt) ©1996, 2004 by Tyndale Charitable Trust. Used by permission of Tyndale House Publishers. All rights reserved.

The Holy Bible, New International Version (niv) ©1973, 1978, 1984, 2011 by Biblica, Inc.™ Used by permission. All rights reserved worldwide.

The Holy Bible, English Standard Version (esv) ©2001 by Crossway Bibles, a division of Good News Publishers. Used by permission. All rights reserved.

Every Navy SEAL on this planet has one thing in common: they first graduated from Basic Underwater Demolition/ SEAL (BUD/S) training in Coronado, California.

During the six months of SEAL training, they're called tadpoles because their forefathers were the famed Navy Frogmen.

To be a tadpole means you haven't rung out, and you hope to be one of the few to graduate BUD/S training. To survive as a tadpole, you have to be physically robust, mentally tenacious, and prepared to die if necessary.

DEDICATION

---

*For the mighty men of Basic Underwater Demolition SEAL (BUD/S)
Training Class 89 with whom I was honored to serve my country.*

CONTENTS

FOREWORD

WE ALL HAD OUR DEMONS while trying to survive Hell Week at BUD/S in Coronado, California, in 1976. Pool training was an exercise where our instructors tied our feet and wrists together and tossed us into the deep end of the pool. Our job was to bob up and down for thirty minutes without drowning.

I was lucky. I was a lifeguard during the summers and felt confident in my ability to make it through. My brother Larry Fowler, on the other hand, was not the best of swimmers. On top of that, he had negative buoyancy. Add the fact that we had not slept in days, and our body temperatures were low, with constant shivering.

I remember watching Larry coughing, gasping for air, and trying to keep his head above water. Frankly, I thought he would surely quit or drown. The instructors were looking for a quitter, and they thought Larry was ripe for giving in. He would clearly rather drown first.

Somehow, someway, he made it through that night. It became an inspiration for me and others who witnessed his fortitude and perseverance. Larry became a shining example of never giving up on your dream. I am proud to call him my great friend and brother!

Hooyah!

—*Scott Rawding, BUD/S Class 89*

"Though a mighty army surrounds me,
My heart will not be afraid.
Even if I am attacked,
I will remain confident."

—Psalm 27:3 (NLT)

INTRODUCTION

Giving Up Everything—and Finding More

"BECOMING A NAVY SEAL IS one of the most selfless acts a man can do, since he must be willing to give up everything." That's how my friend, teammate, and BUD/S Class 89 honor man Doug Young put it. It's arguably the most difficult military warrior training anywhere.

All Navy SEALs on this planet have one thing in common: they first graduated from Basic Underwater Demolition/SEAL (BUD/S) training in Coronado, California. During the six months of SEAL training, candidates are called "tadpoles" because their forefathers were the famed Navy frogmen. To be a tadpole means you haven't rung out, and you hope to be one of the few to graduate BUD/S training. To survive as a tadpole, you must be physically robust, mentally tenacious, and prepared to die if necessary. Those six months can feel like an eternity. The immediate lead-up, however, can be deceptive.

After landing at San Diego International Airport, each trainee drives across the beautiful Coronado Bridge over picturesque San Diego Bay, passing the palm-shaded grounds of the historic Hotel del Coronado (originally the largest resort hotel in the world, where presidents, royalty, and movie stars have come to vacation). He continues for a few minutes down Silver Strand Boulevard to see Coronado Naval Amphibious Base nestled along a beach with gentle waves, calm breezes, and sun-browned bodies on the sand.

Inside the compound, the beauty stops.

Within the ten-foot wire fences, the BUD/S instructors—affectionately called the "Coronado gods"—dominate. This is unequivocally their domain. No one dares argue. As the tenacious gatekeepers of the Navy SEAL community, their job is to weed out anyone unable to meet the ferocious demands of being a SEAL. And they're consumed by the spontaneous and the absurd.

Coronado gods are experts in pushing others to exceed physical limitations and are fluent in psychological warfare. The gravity of their demands is unmatched. To survive requires not only sacrifice and obedience but also relentless commitment.

Storms abound in BUD/S—and I can testify that they made us tadpoles stronger. We became fearless. The Coronado gods saw to that, constantly demanding more than we thought possible. If we didn't perform the impossible, there were consequences. These gods never blinked, and they expected the same from us. They wanted what was best not only *from* us but *for* us. They knew that the more we sweated in training, the less we would bleed on the battlefield (which certainly didn't mean we didn't bleed in training—as you'll discover in the coming pages).

Why would we want to endure all that? Why go through what costs you *everything*?

I believe it's because we were starving for something. We stared down pain and our greatest fears to achieve something greater, something beyond the possible.

We should all be starving for something worthwhile. What are you starving for? What would make you willing to pay whatever price is necessary?

By the time you finish this book, you'll have discovered something valuable about having the courage to live boldly and with abundant purpose—today and for all your tomorrows.

The days that followed my Navy Special Forces days brought

additional storms and personal trials that were more demanding and challenging than anything I had experienced, even in BUD/S. But I'd learned in BUD/S that pushing through the storms was *not* all about strength, size, or ability. What forged tadpoles into future SEALs was heart, attitude, and resolve.

The same is true for every worthwhile challenge awaiting you down the road.

That you are reading this book today is no accident. You were handmade by God not just for *any* purpose, but for His purpose. You have more strength than you know. Live it out.

In life's chaos and darkness, God is writing your story. You get to choose how it ends—beginning now and with every day and every decision that follows.

"The main trouble with despair is that it's self-fulfilling," Norman Cousins pointed out. "People who fear the worst tend to invite it. Heads that are down can't scan the horizon for new openings. A burst of energy does not spring from a spirit of defeat. Ultimately, helplessness leads to hopelessness."[1]

Psychiatrist M. Scott Peck put it another way: "Life is a series of problems. Do we want to moan about them or solve them?"[2]

We get what we expect in life. We must strain every day to find a balance between wisdom and vulnerability to accomplish our goals.

If you're walking through loneliness, anxiety, addiction, loss of a job, anger, lust, greed, suicidal thoughts, a broken relationship, or broken promises—this book is for you. Life's a mess—a beautiful, strange, wonderful mess. As messy as life gets, know that you are wired to thrive through temporary failure—the kind that breeds a lifetime of unfathomable success—transforming you into a warrior.

So suit up, strap in, and brace yourself for new adventures that will take you beyond your comfort zone toward a life of compelling opportunities, impact-resistant strength, and the unbreakable courage every tadpole must know.

1

UNCOMMON COURAGE

Tadpole Faith Is Greater Than Any Fear

"Fowler!" The burly SEAL team instructor's voice echoed off the concrete around us as he called my name. I stepped near the pool's edge. He bent my arms behind my back and tied my wrists together, then my ankles. At his signal, I jumped into the water.

It was 1976, and I was a few weeks into the grueling BUD/S training in Coronado, California. I'd already survived Hell Week—barely—and now I was facing another punishing test: drown-proofing. This exercise requires Navy SEAL trainees to swim 100 meters with their hands bound behind their backs and their ankles tied together.

For a negatively buoyant rock like me, this was bad news. I began a porpoise-like movement to get from one end of the pool to the other, trying not to fill my lungs with too much water. Chlorine poisoning can ruin your day. So can drowning. I could almost hear the BUD/S instructors—the Coronado gods—taking bets on how quickly someone would have to dive in and fish my limp, lifeless body out of the pool.

Surprisingly, I resisted my body's constant desire to sink like a block of granite. Despite my worst fears, I managed to swim all

100 meters—barely. I climbed out of the pool and met the deep, dark gaze of my BUD/S instructor, Senior Chief Ray—six-foot-five and physically ripped because his previous mission in Vietnam required it. His menacing eyes were fixed on the chlorinated blood dripping from my wrists onto his pool deck. The vicious rope cuts from my struggles did not impress him one bit. As the heartless Coronado gods love to say, "Pain is weakness leaving the body."

"Fowler, get over here!" Senior Chief Ray was angry.

He snatched another piece of rope and spun me around, nearly causing me to lose my balance. He quickly retied my wrists and ankles, much tighter this time. I gasped in disbelief as he grabbed yet another piece of rope. In one swift movement, he pulled my elbows together behind my back and tied them too.

As I was still catching my breath, he spat another command. "Repeat the swim, Fowler."

I only vaguely believed he was serious.

"Now!" His voice boomed so loudly, I can still hear it ringing in my ears.

The Navy makes it easy for a tadpole to choose another line of work. In fact, everything about BUD/S is designed to make those who don't belong quit. All you have to do is go to the brass bell, ring it three times—and you're out. No questions asked. A typical BUD/S class begins with about 200 tadpoles, every one a volunteer. On average, about seven percent drop out in pretraining, another twenty-seven percent quit in the first few weeks, and another twenty-one percent ring out during the fourth week, which is Hell Week. By the end of each BUD/S class, three out of every four will have rung that brass bell.

Those who remain will be tested down to the last fiber of their being, confronting every fear. It's about exposing weaknesses so that, with the help of BUD/S instructors and fellow tadpoles, trainees can repurpose those weaknesses into strengths. To survive and graduate, a tadpole must forge an unshakeable resolve not just to survive any storm but also thrive in it.

Senior Chief Ray was my storm that day. If I didn't complete that second swim, I'd never be a SEAL. If I tried, well, rumors abounded of tadpoles drowning in that exact pool throughout the program's history. The danger was real; blackouts were common.

Each of us faces fight-or-flight moments in life. Fear shows up, and we have a decision to make: are we going to persevere, or are we going to panic and ring the bell? Tadpoles are called to push through those fears, to win the race no matter how dire the odds.

I was more determined than ever. I had to learn not to just embrace fear but to thrive in it. I had to accept the fact that I was created to excel. Thriving through fear would no longer be a stranger or distant cousin but who I would become. Tadpoles choose not to panic. They adjust, knowing the situation often commands an immediate response that can lead to panic. They learn to eyeball fear without blinking. They know the past is important, but not nearly as important as today and tomorrow. They make every breath count. To succeed I had to lock in on the finish line.

I took a deep breath into my rope-bound chest. *God had better be real*, I thought, *because I'm either going to finish this swim or meet Him in the midst of it.* Blood dripping from the wounds on my wrists, back into the pool I went.

You would think that the next perilous minutes would have felt like hours, but somehow they went by in a flash. I swam as if in shock. I wrestled with the water just like the first time but with greater intensity. I could see my goal, and I refused to quit. Like an athlete who enters the zone, my body found renewed strength I'd never known before that day. My porpoise-like movements began to even out, propelling me forward on the water's surface.

I was *alive.* I was breathing. As I hauled myself out of the pool, chlorine stinging my shredded skin, I swore I'd never again take for granted the simple act of breathing fresh air.

The Coronado gods know the best predictor of success is

unerring grit and—for a rare few—faith. To recognize God's presence no matter how dire your circumstances is an antidote to fear. But finding such faith is uncommon. All Christ followers who live out their faith will face trials—the enemy's tradecraft is panic, pain, darkness, rejection, greed, bitterness, guilt, unforgiveness, and mediocrity. I call these trials uncommon opportunities. You need uncommon faith to accept these opportunities to refine your confidence, courage, and perseverance. Instead of asking, "Why me?", thank God in advance for the blessings to come. Coach Herb Brooks famously told his 1980 Olympic hockey team before facing the Soviet Union in what many called the upset of the decade, "You cannot be common. The common man goes nowhere; you have to be uncommon."

A tadpole is not a child of mediocrity but of possibilities, created to excel. Always pushing forward, nonstop.

Are you ready to become uncommon, fearless, and as courageous as you'll ever be?

If so, stop bleeding on the deck . . . and get back in the pool.

DARE TO BE COURAGEOUS

- The best predictor of success is grit. How you choose to respond to life's trials—your uncommon moments—is everything.

- Your past is important, but not nearly as important as today and tomorrow.

- Your faith will be sharpened amidst trials, suffering and hardship; and your purpose will become unmistakable.

- Repurpose weaknesses into strengths. When fear threatens to overwhelm you, suck it up and dive in.

- Be the first to volunteer. And don't just meet your fears head on; thrive even in the midst of them.

2

FINDING PURPOSE

Tadpole Faith Believes in a Compelling Purpose

DURING MY SECOND YEAR OF college, I folded slacks and rang up customers at J. Riggings, a menswear store at the local mall. It paid only minimum wage, like most of my previous jobs, but I didn't care. Every paycheck felt like winning the lottery since it was paying for my education (with the help of student loans). As much as I loved cashing those paychecks, I took even more pride in the snazzy wardrobe I could now afford with my employee discount.

I worked hard in my classes, but I played even harder. With my long, wavy bleached-blond hair flowing in the wind, I rode my Kawasaki 500 motorcycle like a daredevil. I didn't care about the bruises and scrapes from a steady stream of crashes. I was a twenty-one year old with a warrior's heart, a reckless spirit, and no direction.

Twenty-one was fun, but I struggled to connect the dots. I had no sense of a life-defining purpose, and it felt like I was on the fast track to nowhere. My life was all about looking good on the outside, but I wasn't fulfilled on the inside. I was overflowing with energy and ambition, but instead of pouncing on opportunities, I circled endlessly like a vulture, unwilling to dive. Nothing felt right. I didn't fit in anywhere.

Many of my friends had embraced the college experience and moved forward in life. I was doing fine in college but never felt like I was thriving. *Was this all life was meant to be?*

I needed a change—big time.

Little did I realize, change was waiting right around the corner.

One day at work I overheard a couple of young men talking about the Navy. Back then, in the mid-1970s, few people—including me—had heard of the SEALs, and I listened eagerly. I learned that Navy SEAL units were a highly specialized force that used unconventional methods and guerrilla tactics in clandestine operations. It reminded me of stories I'd heard about our Revolutionary War when American soldiers and citizens introduced brutal and clever Native American fighting tactics against the English. The English response was, "No fair! You can't fight like *that!*" But it helped change the tide of the war.

That conversation I overheard about the SEALs was a lightning-bolt moment for me. I had to know more. Who exactly were these guys? Were they as strong and daring as they sounded? What did SEAL stand for anyway? The way these guys laughed about their terrifying, painful experiences made me wonder if they were sociopaths. Still, I didn't care. I wanted in.

Eager to explore this new opportunity further, I remembered that my mother had once worked with a Navy recruiter named Jack Lane. I gave Jack a call, and soon he was knocking on our front door. Even before he found a seat at the dining room table, I had a mysterious hunch that my days of feeling lost were over. I thought back to my high school football coach who always screamed at us, "Be somebody!" Jack hadn't said a word yet, but I was determined. I wasn't going to be just *somebody.* I was going to be a Navy SEAL.

Jack wasn't so sure.

"So, what makes you want to join the Navy, son?"

As he sat there listening to me recount what I'd overheard in the clothing store, I watched the light go out of Jack's face. Was it disdain? Discomfort? He continued to listen but with growing disapproval in his sympathetic eyes, as though he didn't know when or how to put an end to my fantasy. For every reason I mentioned for joining the SEALs, Jack—as steady as a seasoned trial attorney—told me five reasons why I should run in the opposite direction. He was aware of the horrific odds of anyone making it through BUD/S.

When he saw I couldn't be warned off so easily, he tried a different approach. During wartime, he explained, practical jokes help break the tension, offering a diversion from the pain and stress of battle. And when it comes to pulling pranks, Navy SEALs are the best—or the worst, depending on which end of the joke you are on.

Back in Vietnam, a SEAL platoon was about to eat when one of the guys found the remains of a rapidly decomposing rat. He happened to be in charge of preparing the team's meal that day, and he decided one of the guys would be served the worst sandwich of his life.

With all but one of these buddies in on the joke, the SEALs sat together in a tight circle. They eagerly looked on as their hapless target bit into his rat sandwich. I can only imagine the feeling of anticipation among the pranksters as he munched on the raw, rotting rat meat. Watching him out of the corners of their anxious eyes, the others could barely wait to burst into laughter the second their buddy lost his lunch.

But that moment never came. The eater of the rat sandwich was no ordinary man. Sure, that first bite went down a little slower than usual, but the second and third bites did not. No look of shock. No throwing up. No anger. Nothing. He just kept on chewing as if that sandwich was a nice juicy slab of filet mignon. He carried on smiling and talking as if nothing was wrong. The rat-eating SEAL won the battle, though he paid for it the moment he was alone. The rat had no problem reintroducing itself to the outside world.

After wrapping up the story, Jack proudly sat back and took a deep breath, as if he'd just played a royal flush on a million-dollar jackpot. He thought he'd dropped a huge damper on my conviction to become a SEAL. *Not even close.* Instead, he'd given me a model to run after—a purpose. I wanted to *be* that rat-eating frogman. I wanted to be the resolute warrior who could choke down a death sandwich with a straight face.

In *Man's Search for Meaning,* Viktor Frankl wrote that whenever his fellow Holocaust prisoners in Auschwitz lost their sense of purpose, they inevitably fell sick and died. The prisoners who held on to their purpose in life were the ones who managed to survive. Frankl's observation has since been proven time and time again. A study of 136,000 participants at St. Luke's-Roosevelt Hospital in New York demonstrated that people with a greater sense of purpose enjoy a lower risk of cardiovascular failure.[3] Similar studies have shown purposeful living to be a strong predictor of happiness as well as a powerful antidote to depression. As if those benefits aren't enough, a heightened sense of purpose leads to improved career satisfaction, higher income, and as much as a *seven-year bump* in life expectancy, according to various studies.

As human beings, there's no greater motivator than finding our purpose in life. In fact, purpose can provide a sense of identity. It's who we are and what others think of us. If you don't know your purpose, the best you can hope to do is drift through life without kicking up too much of a fuss. "The deepest urge in human nature," said American philosopher John Dewey, "is the desire to be important." Your purpose can confidently answer the question of why you exist.

Everyone walking this planet has a compelling God-given purpose. It's unique to *you.* No one else can pull it off. It's yours. It fulfills your deepest need for significance.

And it will never go away.

At twenty-one, I had no idea of what a life-defining purpose should look like. My goals were to chase after the world's view of success: graduate from college, make a ton of money, and have fun. These goals had some degree of worthiness but ultimately could never be more than temporary; they would have eventually left me at sea without a rudder. But now I wanted more in life. Much more.

Despite Jack's attempts to dissuade me, I had a mysterious hunch after talking with him about the SEALs, so I decided to trust my gut. I was ready for a new challenge. In fact, I needed it far more than it needed me.

Risk is never easy, no matter how great the reward. As great as your purpose is, there is always a corresponding sacrifice. Pursuing your purpose doesn't mean you *might* have to eat a rat sandwich or two along the way; it guarantees it. The important thing is to know exactly how to do it.

One bite at a time.

DARE TO FIND YOUR PURPOSE

- Purposeful living is a strong indicator of happiness. Live big. Believe bigger. Thrive always.

- No reward in life comes without sacrifice. Define exactly what you want out of life.

- Live toward a purpose greater than yourself, not as a consumer but as a giver.

- True faith requires a commitment that transforms our every thought.

3

BURN YOUR SHIPS

Tadpole Faith Anticipates and Welcomes Failure

AS YOU'VE HEARD A MILLION times, there are no guarantees in life. Jack, the Navy recruiter, kept drilling that fact into my head. He knew I'd find it far easier to just enroll in the Navy and bypass my dreams of becoming a SEAL. Everyone who enlists in the Navy is promised a school, which leads to a career path in the Navy. If I did make it to BUD/S but then washed out or got seriously injured, I wouldn't be eligible for a career school or job training of any kind. So Jack attempted to sway me to schools that would pay me cash bonuses due to the tremendous need for recruits. He was testing my mettle, but I didn't budge.

"I'm not interested in any schools or careers," I said. "I want to join the Navy for one reason only—to become a SEAL." I leaned back in my chair to convey what I hoped was a more relaxed pose.

Back when I enlisted, the minimum requirements to get into BUD/S were a 500-yard swim, 50 push-ups, 50 sit-ups, 10 pull-ups, and a 1.5-mile run in boots. Each event was timed. Only two out of every ten applicants passed. For me to fail any of those minimum requirements would have serious ramifications for my future in the Navy.

Jack sat in silence, staring at me over his half-moon reading glasses. "Well, all I can offer you is one guaranteed school. Are you certain you want to gamble your entire Navy career on becoming a SEAL with such terrible odds of making it? That's an awfully big risk. If you wash out, you'll be flushing the next four years down the toilet. You need to give this some serious thought."

In truth, I wouldn't just be flushing my life down the toilet; without a school or specialized training, I would be cleaning toilets—literally—as a low-ranking member of the Navy. I knew Jack had my best interests at heart, and I appreciated that he wanted me to succeed. He was a pragmatist who was being upfront about the odds—harsh as they were.

I returned his stare. His words of warning had grabbed my attention, but they hadn't lessened my resolve. My answer jumped out of my mouth. "Okay, I've thought about it. Where do I sign?"

In his classic book *Think and Grow Rich*, Napoleon Hill shares a well-known story about the conquistador Hernán Cortés, who arrived with two ships to attack an island. The enemy greatly outnumbered his army. Before attacking, and with the odds overwhelmingly against them, Cortés ordered his men to burn the two ships on which they'd arrived. The small battalion would either succeed or die trying; retreat was not an option. I didn't realize until much later how this Cortés story mirrored my mindset in interacting with Jack. He wanted to snuff out my spark of excitement to become a SEAL, but instead, he fanned it into a flame. *I was willing to burn my ships.*

What I came to realize later was how much we're all called to burn our ships every day. Life's a mess. Success comes with a price. Relationships test our resolve. It's not just about finding purpose or significance but finding a purpose that's worth burning our ships—a purpose that will cause you to live bigger, bolder, and beyond yourself.

Living stronger also means embracing *every* failure. As my friend Zig Ziglar once said, "Failure is an event and never the person." The truth is, failure's nothing more than an opportunity for greater success. Adversity introduces a man to himself. Show me a great father, CEO, or warrior, and I'll show you someone who never rings out when confronted by failure but instead faces the challenge. If you haven't already, learn to see failure as God's greatest opportunity to do greater things in your life.

My conversation with Jack only increased my motivation to survive BUD/S. With a profound but ironic sense of gratitude to Jack, the threat of cleaning toilets for the next four years gave me the extra burst of strength I would need to endure the pain that was to come.

And the days to come would be painful indeed.

DARE TO RISK EVERYTHING

- You win a few, and you learn from a few. Always remember failure is necessary for growth. Embrace it; don't run from it.
- Don't blink at the first hint of failure. Keep going with an all-in, all the time attitude.
- All great accomplishments require self-sacrificing commitment while knowing failure is possible and imminent.

4

THE HEART OF A NAVY SEAL

Tadpole Faith Makes Others Feel Important

I WAS SO GEARED UP to start the new life I'd envisioned that I arrived at Navy boot camp in Orlando, Florida, thinking it was a complete waste of time. Merely a box to check off on my way to BUD/S training. Going anywhere except Coronado felt like a hindrance.

My only goal at boot camp was to gain permission to take the BUD/S qualification test. I didn't have the brains to realize it was also my opportunity to become accustomed to military discipline, learn Navy procedures and culture, and, of course, get myself a handsome haircut.

In my mind I was already fit to pass the BUD/S required qualification test, so I figured it would be a piece of cake. After all, I had extremely low body fat. I was five feet, eleven inches tall and weighed 155 pounds. Moreover, I'd earned football honors in high school, and I once led my school's physical training class in doing more than 500 sit-ups.

You are probably thinking that I was pretty full of myself—which is an understatement. Even so, I was not at all prepared for what was coming at me.

Several weeks after arriving at boot camp, the big day arrived, the one for which I'd burned my ships. I confidently walked to the base gym with my chest pumped and feeling confident. I checked in with Master Chief Saunders, the first real Navy SEAL I'd ever officially met. He was of average height, but he strutted about like a peacock, his head held high. Although he wasn't the highest-ranking person in the gym, it was mind-blowing to see how the waters parted wherever this man walked.

I noticed his Navy SEAL trident—also known as the Budweiser medal—worn proudly on his chest above his many war ribbons. Admittedly, I already felt intimidated.

Master Chief Saunders stared into my eyes and I into his. I blinked. Somehow my confidence began fading like a slow tire leak. Flashes of anxiety showed up unannounced and uninvited. This was the man who'd oversee the physical test to determine if I qualified to go to BUD/S training. He held my destiny in his hands.

I had to remind myself to remain focused. After all, this was only a screening test, and I'd passed many similar ones in the past. No big deal.

First, I did the fifty push-ups in the time required, then the fifty sit-ups, the ten pull-ups, and the one-and-a-half mile run wearing boots. I passed them all with time to spare. My confidence could barely be contained.

And then I did the swim.

And failed.

I'd never swum 500 yards in a timed swim before. Apparently, at our local pool during my high school days, I spent too much time admiring the scenery and not enough time swimming.

As I climbed out of the pool, I felt like a wet noodle. Master Chief Saunders stared into my beaten soul as if he knew I'd given my all—which wasn't nearly good enough.

"No problem," he told me, waving it off. "You can retake the test one more time."

I fought to remain optimistic, but discouragement began to creep in for the first time.

I found out the hard way that I had "negative buoyancy" and no glide in my strokes—only the struggle against sinking. I'd have to increase my effort just to stay above water, never mind moving forward. And that effort would only increase my fatigue.

I was doomed. A three-toed sloth could swim faster than me.

Should I have listened to Jack? Would I be mopping decks for the next four years? My heart began to pound as my future passed before my eyes. It included a lot of toilets.

Just like that, my vision of going to Coronado and becoming a Navy SEAL began to waver and fade.

Several days later, I reported to Master Chief Saunders to re-take the entire test. Time to do or die. I was so anxious, I thought I might faint. I'd never doubted myself as much as at that moment. Though I struggled to remain hopeful, fear began seeping in. I could feel the vultures circling. My drug of choice was doubt, but I had no other option. There was no turning back. My four-year Navy contract was signed, a done deal.

It was sink or swim. Literally.

Just like before, I easily passed the running, the push-ups, the sit-ups, and the pull-ups. Once again, only swimming could be my downfall.

When it was time to get into the pool, Master Chief Saunders watched my every move. I supposed that, as the gatekeeper to BUD/S, he gave everyone this intense hellacious once-over, like a father eyeing his daughter's first date.

"Go!" he shouted, with little time for me to prepare mentally. The evil stopwatch gripped firmly in his hand began to tick.

I gave it everything I had. In that pool, 500 yards was 5 laps—it was like swimming 5 football fields. The first couple of laps, I felt like Michael Phelps. By the third my arms began to feel like cement blocks. With every stroke, my lungs burned, and I gasped for air. I'd lost feeling in my legs, and I still had a couple of laps to go.

When I completed lap three, I had nothing left in the tank.

After the fourth lap, whatever faint hope I'd possessed had departed.

I'm not sure how I finished that fifth and last lap, but when I pushed to touch the wall, I almost collapsed. After struggling to climb out of the pool, I could barely stand. I'd experienced plenty of grueling runs and drills in football training in high school and college, but I'd never been so physically depleted. And although I'd invested my heart and soul in the swim, I knew I couldn't have come in under the required time. I'd wagered the next four years of my life—and lost.

I closed my eyes and saw my life flashing by.

As I gasped for breath, I didn't have the courage or the strength to look up at the master chief. When I finally did, Master Chief Saunders stared at me for a long moment, as if looking beyond, deep into my soul. Finally, with a fierce expression, he told me I'd passed.

I thought I'd experienced a miracle. Then a terrible thought crossed my mind. Could he be pulling a prank, like the SEALs in the rat sandwich story? As I wavered on my feet, I saw he wasn't smiling. It was no joke.

To this day, I don't believe I beat the clock with that swim. I think maybe Master Chief Saunders went above and beyond and chose to invest in me despite my failure. Maybe he knew that sometimes failure is just an event, not a person. Maybe he knew that even though my swim didn't measure up to Navy SEAL standards on the clock, it hit the mark in a more important way, in a place where it counted more—in the heart and soul.

If that's the case (and I believe it is), he taught me not to judge people by their abilities but by their hearts. Now, decades later, I believe you can measure the joy in a person's life by the amount of joy they invest in others. As Napoleon once said, "Leaders are dealers of hope." I think also of Ronald Reagan, who as governor of California received a letter from a soldier serving in Vietnam asking if he'd call the soldier's wife to wish her happy anniversary on his behalf. Secretly, and without any fanfare, Reagan showed up at the soldier's house and delivered flowers on the soldier's behalf—and spent almost a full hour visiting with the soldier's wife and family.

Maybe Master Chief Saunders noticed something in me that I'd never seen before. Great people do that. They naturally see beyond and make others feel important.

Master Chief Saunders has since passed away, but if I could thank him, I would. I do, however, thank God every day that Saunders took account of my intent and my effort rather than merely judging me by my performance.

Since then I've made it my life's mission to pass on the same type of grace to others. When I graduated from Navy boot camp, my sixty or so peers in my company nominated me for honor recruit. I'd like to think their tribute resulted from my applying what I'd learned from Master Chief Saunders to my fellow recruits.

After boot camp, I received my orders to go to BUD/S. Burning my ships had paid off, but I was still a long, long way from becoming a Navy SEAL. And when I arrived at Coronado, I was in for the surprise of my life. I'd need more than a miracle from Master Chief Saunders. I would need a miracle from God.

DARE TO MAKE OTHERS FEEL IMPORTANT

- People who love big are constantly reaching out to others. Always speak to others first whenever appropriate. When we talk more than we listen, we're telling others our opinions are more important than theirs.

- Love all others no matter the circumstances, not because of who or what they are but because of who you are. Active loving is our litmus test of true faith.

- Success is measured by the amount of joy you invest in others. Look for the best in others, even when it's obscured. Positivity begets more positivity.

- Embrace JOY (Jesus, Others, Yourself, in that order) today.

5

BUILD YOUR MASTERMIND TEAM

Tadpole Faith Is the Iron That Sharpens Iron

Since I knew BUD/S started a new class every few months, I flew to San Diego a month or so early, allowing me plenty of time to get into top physical condition before training began. I knew I had to work hard on swimming, especially in cold water. While the sea and sandy beaches in San Diego look warm and appealing, the average yearly temperature of the water is a mere 55°F. Of course, it feels much colder without a wetsuit, and enduring the frigid temperatures, especially during winter, adds another level of stress for incoming recruits.

When I checked in at the base at Coronado, I discovered I wouldn't have the preparation time I anticipated. A new BUD/S class was just starting, and they needed a few more warm bodies to fill out the roster. From their perspective, I'd arrived just in time. From my perspective, I was doomed. I'd finished basic training only a week earlier, and—no offense to the Navy—that training was incapable of getting anyone physically prepared for the exhausting ordeal of BUD/S.

Any veteran will tell you that the needs of the military always come first. And so, just like that, my nightmare began. Most of the other tadpoles in BUD/S Class 89 were already hard-body physical robots, conditioned long-distance runners, and faster-than-shark swimmers—everything I wasn't. Many had prepared for months, watching and learning from previous BUD/S classes. There were also a few "rollbacks" who'd been injured in an earlier class and sent to our class. Thankfully, rather than mock or belittle me for my lack of physical conditioning right out of basic boot camp, a few of my fellow tadpoles—who became lifelong friends—were quick to offer me encouragement and reassurance, which gave this Georgia boy hope.

For the first phase of BUD/S, every day began with physical training. The wake-up call was at 4:30 a.m. With boots tightly tied, tadpoles ran to breakfast in squads of six or seven team members while carrying a boat on their heads. Though inflatable, the boats were still heavy. (One time, as punishment, we had to carry our boat with one of our BUD/S instructors riding inside—it was Medal of Honor awardee Michael Thornton, whose weight matched his Mount Everest–sized confidence.)

When our boat squad came in last in yet another race, Senior Chief Ray asked all fifty or so BUD/S Class 89 tadpoles if any of us liked chewing tobacco. He never went anywhere without a plug of tobacco in his cheek. Of course, we all said yes because we said yes to anything the Coronado gods asked, especially when saying no often resulted in Senior Chief Ray spitting a stream of tobacco juice onto our boots.

"Good!" he replied. He pulled the brown wad out of his cheek and handed it to the first tadpole and told him to start chewing. After him, the plug was passed down the line, so every tadpole could take a turn.

By the time it found its way to the last tadpole, it didn't smell as bad (or maybe I was hallucinating), but it was nearly impossible to chew without gagging. Most of us left everything we'd eaten that day on the beach.

Through that experience, in some strange way, we bonded.

Each day in phase one we focused on three main "evolutions," or training segments. Some days this involved the O Course, an incredibly difficult obstacle course set up on the beach, a stone's throw from gentle waves and sunbathers basking in the Southern California sunshine. The course confronted us with such obstacles as the diabolical "low wall" (at least eight feet high), a barbed-wire obstacle, logs we had to run across while they rolled back and forth, and the "spider wall"—a series of log vaults that included a web of thick ropes.

The first obstacle on the course was called the "belly buster," a series of five horizontal log rails set up four feet apart and getting successively higher, with the first at ground level and the last about nine feet high. We were expected to leap from log to log all the way to the highest rail. One of my best pals had trouble on this one due to his short stature, and he ended up cracking a rib. Even after recovering, he couldn't get through it. He finally went out one night and tried again and again, without success. Then a guy from an earlier class came and showed him that if he leaped a little differently, he might manage better. It worked. His tenacity paid off, and he triumphed over the belly buster.

Running the timed O Course as well as our usual beach runs in the thick sand that built up on the bottom of our combat boots was unmatched by anything I'd previously experienced. But "log PT" was one of the most physically draining exercises imaginable. Squads of six or seven men had to cart around a telephone pole that weighed 400 to 600 pounds. We hoisted it onto our shoulders and moved right, then left, then lifted it above our heads, then did sit-ups with it cradled in our laps, then walked with it between our legs—whatever evil task the Coronado gods could come up with.

Each day after our final evolution, I ate dinner and went straight to bed. I didn't read the newspaper, make phone calls, or socialize. My priority was taking care of my beaten body. If I saw a sunset, it was well past my normal bedtime.

Our later phase of training included an even worse exercise

than log PT. Called the "iron butterfly," it had nothing to do with the 1960s classic rock band and everything to do with pain. On each of our backs the Coronado gods would place a wooden or steel pallet weighing around seventy pounds. Carrying it, we had to run—not walk—up and back down a nearby hill, which was really a small mountain. Rocks and pebbles could trip you up. It was a wonder no one broke a leg (in our class, at least). Like airplanes, we had to keep circling until we had permission to "land." If the Coronado gods didn't like the look of our "flight," they made us do it all over again.

What did drills like that create besides trembling arms and perspiring brows? *Teamwork.* The most important factor in the majority of our training exercises was learning to work as a team. Every tadpole was expected to pull, carry, or lug his own weight, not only for himself but also for the good of the team. If we had a slacker in our boat crew, it meant everybody else had to carry the extra weight. And everybody on the crew knew who was pulling their weight and who wasn't. Such pressure helped build a tight camaraderie, because to get through tough training drills like log PT, we had to trust each other in a whole new way, working together more than ever.

Most BUD/S evolutions were designed so that no one could survive on his own. Team effort was everything. Boat races from the shore through the explosive Pacific surf were brutal tasks for every crew. It was the ultimate gut test of teamwork. The only way to break through the mountainous crashing waves and reach the calm water beyond was to row in perfect tandem. The formidable waves often ripped a boat crew in half, sending paddles and bodies flying. One team member off-sync could jeopardize the entire crew.

Although deaths do occur during BUD/S training, the number of fatalities was not made public back then. Every event was a race, and both the Coronado gods and our fellow tadpoles demanded maximum effort. The danger of landing our boats on massive sharp-edged rocks in total darkness exposed hidden fears and forced boat crews to work as a team.

During one evolution at dawn, having had no sleep, we set our course into Coronado Bay. The job of our officer in the stern was to man the rudder while our boat crew dug in and paddled. We seemed to row forever until finally we ran aground. The officer had fallen asleep with his steering paddle locked into place while the rest of us—glassy-eyed and dazed from lack of sleep—had stared unseeingly forward, mechanically dipping our paddles in unison for what seemed like hours. Once aground we collected ourselves and set out again.

Admittedly, I was among the worst-performing prospects in Class 89. A three-legged elephant would have had a better running stride than I did, and I swam like a dead mosquito. Fortunately, whenever I struggled, my teammates were there to cheer me along, lift me up, and drag me forward.

At BUD/S, we were all assigned a swim buddy, someone to stay right beside us—within six feet or else—throughout every phase of training. Without Guy Cortise, my swim buddy, and without Scotty, Doug, Spencer, Mr. Payne, and all the rest of Class 89, I would never have made it. Whenever I was given the opportunity—when I could hold my head above water long enough, that is—I did what I could to help them. For all of us, lifting others up became a way of life, a culture. It wasn't just expected; it was demanded if we wanted to become Navy SEALs.

One day we were dropped off in the Pacific and instructed to swim through open ocean back to shore. I started to lose control of my arms and noticed signs of hypothermia. I wanted to keep going, but my training officer ordered my swim partner and me out of the water. I was taken straight to the hospital, where, in addition to hypothermia, I was diagnosed with a mild flu. Not wanting us to miss out on the pleasures of that particular exercise, the Coronado gods ordered Guy and me to redo the swim the following Saturday while our fellow tadpoles had the day off. I don't think Guy ever forgave me.

Despite that, whenever I finished a run or a swim in the back of the class, as I often did, Guy encouraged me to keep going. During the long runs, especially the fourteen-miler, he lifted my spirits with songs. He provided a directional compass toward whatever it would take to succeed. I came to regard Guy and my boat crew as my "mastermind group." Not only did they give me encouragement when my confidence was lacking, but they also held me accountable to my commitments, and I did the same for them.

Motivated by love, mastermind groups encourage and challenge each other when times are tough. They learn when to offer each other a friendly kick in the pants and when to be strong for each other. Doing this requires self-sacrifice and a genuine investment in each other. That can be hard in today's culture of self-enrichment and selfish gain. Who has time anymore to focus on the needs of others? However, everyone should have a mastermind group they meet with regularly. Get started by finding a close friend and accountability partner who can become your "swim buddy" in life.

In BUD/S training, my swim buddy, Guy, stoked my inner fire to become a winner. This man was always turbocharged and in my face to keep me motivated to complete each evolution. He reminded me to take one evolution at a time. He was there to jet propel me when I was down and to get between me and the bell if I was tempted to give up. If we were on a four-mile ocean swim and I began to suck water, he had two choices: carry me on his back, or suck water and drown with me. I'll never know what I did for Guy, but I do know my trust in and unnerving commitment to us was unwavering. The two of us became one. We knew we would succeed or fail together.

I still need a swim buddy. After BUD/S, I found that trials rarely take a vacation. In a fallen world, life continues to bring difficulties. For helping you through those tough times, your swim buddy can be a friend, a sibling, your spouse, or your pastor. All that's required is someone who can keep his or her head above water, someone who isn't drowning already and in danger of pulling you down with them. It's alright to help such people, but when it comes to the long haul, choose a swim buddy who can match you stroke for stroke, so you can continue to encourage each other as you move toward your destination.

A real swim buddy will be at your side on a moment's notice—just as our BUD/S swim buddies were never more than six feet away. Nothing will hold him or her back but God Himself. Over the forty years since BUD/S, Guy has never been more than a phone call away, and we're always ready to drop whatever we're doing to help each other.

Once you have your swim buddy, expand your mastermind group, like a boat crew prepared to roar through the turbulent ocean waves. Connect with a larger group of trusted individuals, close friends who hold each other accountable to values and goals and who encourage each other to be the best they can be. That's what my fellow tadpoles and I did. We didn't compromise or take shortcuts; we stuck together and relied on each other throughout some pretty harrowing circumstances. We went full throttle with each other and for each other. For a Navy SEAL, going full throttle isn't just for a season or just for a BUD/S class; it's a lifestyle. It's a forward-thinking mindset and a fearless attitude.

During BUD/S, the Coronado gods were surgical about removing tadpoles who were "sappers"—those who sap energy from others instead of strengthening the team. You know the type. They're the ones who seem to always run out of runway before they get up enough speed to get off the ground. In life, sappers are everywhere. If you're not careful, sappers will use you as a continuous dumping ground, dropping most of their problems onto you.

So choose your mastermind group wisely. Don't allow just anyone into your inner circle. Proverbs 13:20 says, "Walk with the wise and become wise; associate with fools and get in trouble"

(NLT). Instead of hanging out with lazy people, choose go-getters as your friends, people who produce rather than merely consume. Create a circle of friends who are determined to excel. The more friends you have who succeed, the more likely you are to live a life that transcends the norm, like that of a Navy SEAL.

The book of Proverbs also tells us, "As iron sharpens iron, so one person sharpens another" (27:17, NIV). If your close friends live a purpose-driven life, so will you. As my dear friend Jared Faellaci tells his children, "Show me your friends, and I'll show you your future."

As individuals, we all have various strengths and abilities, but as I learned quickly in BUD/S training, we can make it only so far on our own. So be intentional about finding a swim buddy and forming a mastermind group, and get ready to soar. God created you and me to be relational beings, but I know how easy it is to get trapped in my own comfort zone, becoming lazy about building healthy new relationships or maintaining existing ones.

Becoming a team player may require us to push outside the boundaries of our comfort zone. But as any tadpole knows, the further we get outside our comfort zone, the more we grow. As Jack Canfield said, "Consider your comfort zone as a prison you live in." One thing is for sure: we rarely achieve anything of importance within our comfort zone. So get going. No excuses for any tadpole or you.

There's no doubt about it, this world needs courageous men and women who dare to live abundantly. Be a forward thinker, and become a light for others. Adopt the faith of a daring tadpole as your own. Once you do, you'll be ready for Hell Week.

DARE TO BUILD A MASTERMIND TEAM

- Don't allow yourself to live in a prison cell of a comfort zone.
- Find a community of people who bring out the best in you and build relationships with them.
- A mastermind team excels by raising the communal bar. Keep wise people around you who have similar goals. Iron sharpens iron.

6

GENTLEMEN, IT'S GOING TO BE A LONG, COLD, WET NIGHT

Tadpole Faith Always Runs the Race to Win

FROM WATER TORTURE TO PHYSICAL and mental abuse, from undesired body restructuring to extreme sleep deprivation, Hell Week at BUD/S was the final step between phase one and phase two of our training. The time had come to see who really wanted to pay the price of becoming a Navy SEAL—the ones who would rather die than quit.

Hell Week was the ultimate gut check, a scripted plan of utter chaos to test our ability to maintain resolve under pressure. It wasn't about personal achievement; it was about teamwork, commitment, and heart. To survive, we had to become numb to misery. Five and a half days of pain in exchange for a lifetime of pride.

Hell Week started on Sunday at about five o'clock in the afternoon with a breakout of loud gunfire and flash grenades. For the first three days, we got no sleep at all. On the fourth and fifth days, we got one to two hours of sleep a day. So by the end of the week, we'd had a total of three to four hours of sleep. Meanwhile, we ran more than 200 miles and did physical training for more than 20 hours a day. Someone estimated that tadpoles expend

7,000 calories a day. With that much exertion, ninety-six hours of sleep deprivation created havoc in our bodies and minds. For some, the mental and physical trauma never faded away.

Almost every evolution during Hell Week was designed to spark delusion and confusion. Every tadpole was tested for his commitment in the face of pain and physical limitations. Being cold, wet, and miserable destroyed our confidence. The goal was for us to turn all our cold-water misery and physical pain into aggression. For those who succeeded, the reward was more pain, more cold, more wetness, and more misery. If someone allowed himself to question whether he could succeed, the deadly "mind serpent" would likely appear, and it was only a matter of time before its poisonous fangs sank into the tadpole's resolve, and he rang the bell.

One of the exercises at the beginning of Hell Week was a timed four-mile run in which we were expected to post a personal best. Then, after seventy-two grueling hours of excruciating around-the-clock evolutions and no sleep, we were ordered to do the run again; and the Coronado gods warned us that if we didn't beat our previous time, we would be kicked out. The mental hit was so devastating, many of the guys simply rang out without even trying. As for the rest of us, I'm not sure if anyone posted a new personal best, but many of us came close. Fear of losing our spot gave us an extra push around each corner of the track. That was what the Coronado gods were looking for—they were never really going to kick us out, but we didn't know that.

During the third or fourth day of Hell Week, we paddled several hours in our beloved inflatable boats from Coronado down the coast to the infamous mudflats in Tijuana, Mexico, a distance of about ten miles. Once there, we quickly learned the word *mud* was a euphemism for something far more nefarious: raw sewage. The smell alone was enough to make us gag.

Over the next twelve hours, we were submerged in three to four feet of decayed human waste, direct from Tijuana. We had to do somersaults across the black muck, swim through it, and crawl through it like submerged caterpillars, all the while singing songs at the top of our lungs.

We were wet, freezing, and filthy beyond imagination. It was so cold in the middle of the night that the definition of a good swim buddy during such moments became one who was willing to express his warm urine on his partner. Trust me, in such moments you'll do whatever it takes to feel even a fleeting moment of warmth. The fact that BUD/S no longer sends tadpoles to the Tijuana mudflats should tell you just how vile it was.

One of the training evolutions we had to carry out in the mudflats was brain-dead simple: avoid getting caught by the Coronado gods. It was something like capture the flag, minus the flag. A full day and night of sleepless "games" up to our armpits— and when hiding, up to our hairlines—in black human waste. This Tijuana experience left my body somewhat different than it was when we began.

During the first of three medical checkups we were required to have each day during Hell Week, the medic noticed something strange about my nether regions. Since I was on "automatic," either I hadn't noticed, or I'd noticed but couldn't bring myself to care.

Let me explain "automatic" to you. It's a mental switch your mind flicks on your behalf to put you into survival mode. The pain becomes less intense. Lack of sleep no longer has the power to paralyze your hopes. Your limbs tremble, and your eyes feel like sandpaper, but if you want to succeed, you ignore the pain, weariness, and confusion and keep moving forward. You become a bustling zombie, following orders without thinking. If pain, cold water, or physical hostilities overthrow your body, it doesn't matter. You just go. It's a desired state of mind for a tadpole, similar to the "zone" for an athlete. And I was there.

Back to the checkup—it turns out that certain bacteria found in human waste can cause selected personal parts of a man's body to swell, like barbell weights hanging off his body. I found that out the hard way when I dropped my shorts that morning for the doctor and revealed my new heavenly belongings. Gargantuan is not the right word, but it's pretty close. Swimming in the Tijuana mudflats all night had led to an infection that caused my testicles to expand to the size of grapefruits. The sight was too much for one Coronado god, Chief Gardner. As I disrobed, he took one look and then whipped his head away. I thought he was going to vomit.

The Navy medic advised me to go to the hospital immediately. However, it was day four of Hell Week, not to mention practically the end of the mudflats, and frankly, as horrifying as I looked, I was not feeling any pain. Being on automatic was a definite gift from above! I refused to go to the hospital and committed to staying with my boat crew—my mastermind group—to the end. I would not let this "little" setback distract me from my immediate goal of surviving Hell Week. I remained resolved, focused, and committed. I wasn't dead, so I couldn't quit.

I believe that was the moment the Coronado gods finally saw something special in this Southern boy who, until then, could barely keep his head above water. Who knows? Maybe they have hearts after all. But there was no denying I had the one thing required of every Navy SEAL.

Balls.

Both figurative and literal.

Quitting was not an option for me. Going on automatic enabled me to ignore the pain and misery and to toss out any anxieties I might have allowed to creep in otherwise.

I still go on automatic today, especially during life's storms. I know what it's like to lose a business. I've experienced firsthand what it feels like to have no food. I understand the pain of financial stress, anxiety, disappointments from friends and family, and worst of all, losing a child. I've journeyed down many paths that have created incredibly painful memories that will remain with me for the rest of my life. But rather than numbing my body or emptying my mind during such circumstances, I simply surrender my mind to God and allow His Spirit to fill me. Instead of the situation tearing at my self-confidence and tempting me to ring out, I can keep moving forward, no matter what life brings to bear.

Do I feel pain? Yes, but I decide what to do with it rather than let it dictate my life. It's a choice you have to make. Hurt feelings filled with emotional baggage can be a deep, dark, bottomless pit if you indulge them. Just like Hell Week, nothing lasts forever. If you're not in the midst of a storm right now, that means one is on its way. During the most tragic of storms, we must remain resolved to find the inversely proportional benefit. No matter how bad the circumstance, God's presence and His purpose reign.

During times of trouble, go on *automatic* like a tadpole in training. Hold steadfast. Don't fear the pain; embrace it. Bad things happen, but you always have a choice: either go beyond the mental mudflats, or get stuck in the black muck. Moving forward is far better than remaining where you are—or worse, ringing out on life's defining moments. Every tadpole knows that nothing worthwhile comes easily. There'll be pain, sadness, and heartache. People will disappoint you. Such things are part of life. You must never give up.

I love the story about an air show performer test pilot named Bob Hoover. During a show, he was flying his death-defying air stunts at a mere 300 feet when suddenly his engines went dead. He instinctively went into SOS mode and magically landed his plane in the nearest field. He soon discovered his plane got the wrong fuel prior to the show. He hunted down the mechanic who fueled his plane and whose mistake could easily have ended Hoover's life. Instead of criticizing the young man, he saw the opportunity to touch the man's life. "To show you I'm sure you'll never do this again," Hoover said, "I want you to service my plane tomorrow."

No matter the circumstances, God is bigger than your greatest storm. As author and teacher Christine Caine says, "You don't have to live in defeat, you don't have to live in doubt, you don't have to be insecure. What Satan created will not define me."[4] Courageous people understand that each situation commands a response, but at the same time they accept not being in control of everything. This means not stressing out at every curveball. They're always flexible. Our Father doesn't promise to eliminate our trials, but He does offer us the opportunity to grow through them.

As the Coronado gods often reminded us during our endless races, run the race to win; second place is first place for losers.

DARE TO RUN THE RACE TO WIN

- How you respond to life's challenges is everything. When you are overwhelmed, can you go on automatic and release all your concerns to God?

- Tadpoles learn to thrive on being told they can't do something—it's a challenge that fuels success.

- Tadpoles don't panic; they adjust. Be an anchor in every storm, able to eyeball fear and not blink.

- God will give us the strength to fulfill His purpose in us, every time. Be strong, relying not on your own power, but His.

7

THERE ARE NO TIME-OUTS IN WAR

Tadpole Faith Demands Excellence

COLD PACIFIC WATER CAN MAKE a coward of almost anyone.

Phase one of BUD/S was all about our becoming mentally and physically tough and demonstrating whether we were fortunate enough to survive—unwaveringly resolute. Every day we were hit left and right with pain to body parts we didn't even know existed. And if anybody's parts were missed, the Coronado gods were sure to hit them in a subsequent evolution, accompanied by a never-ending stream of verbal harassment. Nothing we did was ever good enough for the instructors. They punished us day and night and expected us to come out of it smiling and singing. And when we managed to excel, we were punished for having held back earlier.

Back then our instructors were pretty much given free rein in their training practices. They had few real guidelines or rules to follow. They could do virtually whatever they wanted with us, and sometimes people got hurt. For the most part, the instructors were Vietnam veterans and were understandably a little more intense than typical military men. It must have been difficult for some of them to have gone through what they experienced and not struggle with PTSD. They were still living on the edge. Sometimes they went *over* the edge as well, but that's the kind of guys they were—the best of the best at a time when few people even knew the SEAL program existed.

What none of the Coronado gods tolerated were excuses. They demanded no matter how dire the situation. If a tadpole whined or complained, he was out. Simple as that. There are no time-outs in war, and the instructors wanted men who could be trusted and relied upon in battle. Their standard was understandable, considering they'd just returned from a war zone.

For those who couldn't hack it, that brass bell was hanging outside the instructors' office, where any SEAL tadpole could ring out when he'd had enough. Then he would lay down his BUD/S helmet on the walkway under the bell. Every day brought more helmets in an ever-longer row.

Studies have sought to uncover why some men quit BUD/S and others don't, but there are no constants as to a person's size, strength, physical ability, or education. In my opinion, it all comes down to heart—a desire to be the best and an unnerving passion to exceed ordinary. Yes, physical and mental fortitude are absolute musts; but if you don't have grit, a spirited attitude, and a tolerance for pain, you won't make it.

The first three weeks of phase one were a massive gut check in all these areas. The class size dropped significantly every day. For those of us who stuck around, if we didn't perform to the expectations of our Coronado gods, we got to sit in cold water. It could happen any time, often by going out and hitting the surf and becoming a sugar cookie (wet and sandy from head to toe) or by submerging ourselves in a tank of cold seawater kept on hand for such purposes. The sand chafed our skin until walking was painful, and running was unbearable. Sometimes we walked with our abraded legs so far apart we looked like bowlegged bronco riders dressed in combat fatigues. Some of us also had to have our penises wrapped in gauze or tape. We took a deep breath when the medic assigned to do the job snipped off the end of the gauze, so we could relieve ourselves.

When cold, the last thing we wanted to do was to get colder. Cold water has no mercy.

I love what Billy Graham once said about getting through tough times: "The mountaintops are great for viewing, but we grow in the valleys." For tadpoles, those valleys were deep in the Pacific.

During each of the three training phases at BUD/S, there was a vast difference in the physical fitness of the tadpoles. The almost 200 phase-one tadpoles were clearly less physically fit than the 30 or so tadpoles who remained during phase two. These phase-two tadpoles, having survived six weeks of horrendous PT and Hell Week, were ripped with clearly defined muscles. Phase-three tadpoles were in the best physical condition possible for a human being. They could run the O Course with their eyes closed, do two hours of PT in a single breath, and run a hundred miles down the beach without breaking a sweat. Okay, that's a little exaggeration, but you get the picture. Phase-three tadpoles strive for excellence, and that means being pure and complete in their desire to not just succeed but radically excel. This requires extraordinary, ongoing conditioning of mind, body, and spirit. Boldness thick enough to stick a knife into.

Confidence is the fuel needed to do this. People are not born thinking this way but are chiseled out from hard work, sacrifice, and commitment to excellence in everything they do, no matter how minimal or huge a task may be. They dare to learn by striving for perfection, nurturing their faith, preparing for success, and having the confidence to embrace failure. In his book *The Naked CEO*, Alex Malley writes, "The only way to build confidence is to take a risk and take action despite your fear of failure, messing up, or embarrassment."[5]

All successful tadpoles know that how you respond to life's delicate moments is everything.

In the movie *Remember the Titans,* Coach Boone (played by Denzel Washington) fiercely lectures his high school football players: "We will be perfect every day and in every aspect of the game. You drop a pass, you run a mile. You miss a blocking assignment, you run a mile. You fumble the football, and I will break my foot off in your John Brown hind parts, and then you will run a mile. Perfection! Let's get to work."[6]

Whatever we strive for in life, we should always demand excellence from ourselves. It's not only a lifestyle but an attitude we respect when we see it in others. The strong don't become rattled, angry, or anxious whenever goals are not achieved. They learn from their mistakes. They see failure as an event *necessary* to getting better and as an opportunity to learn and become stronger.

Tadpole faith also means being prepared. One of my favorite signs in my office says this: "Prior Preparation Prevents Poor Performance." Without such preparation in life, people fail. If soldiers fail to prepare in war, people die.

Every year, thousands line up to run with the bulls in Pamplona, Spain. There are always injuries. Ambulances line the streets. In a recent run, a twenty-two-year-old American was gored to death within thirty seconds of the start.

Like a business or anything else worthwhile, to succeed you must do your homework. It doesn't do any good to just show up, tie your laces, and sprint to your death. The truth is, the five percent who are pros at Pamplona have studied and prepared; they know how to avoid being stampeded by other runners or worse, gored by angry bulls. They know to avoid the drunk amateurs who trip and fall, causing a domino effect for other amateur runners. The pros know that if they do fall, it's best to stay down since the bulls don't want to fall either; they'll jump over you. The pros know the half-mile course well, and they know to avoid the few areas where the majority of injuries occur. And since every runner wears a white shirt and pants with a red sash, the pros also know to tie their sash in a slip knot, in case a furious bull tangles his horn in it.

Even our best-prepared plans can fail. In these moments we must stand resolved. Tadpoles are always flexible. They don't panic; they adjust. They don't stress out at every curveball but stay steadfastly attentive, eagerly awaiting the next pitch—or the next stampeding bull.

DARE TO DEMAND EXCELLENCE OF YOURSELF

- Don't be ordinary; strive for extraordinary. Demand excellence in everything.
- Know sacrifice is necessary. No matter the odds, suck it up, work hard, and push forward.
- Be all-in, all the time, with energy and enthusiasm. Have an "I can do anything" attitude. And believe it.

8

TWO WAYS TO DO SOMETHING: THE RIGHT WAY AND AGAIN

Tadpole Faith Is More Excited about the Journey Than the Destination

LIFE CAN CHANGE FROM GOOD to bad to worst in an instant.

During Hell Week, we were hiding in the mudflats when a BUD/S tadpole we'll call Jones* was captured by the Coronado gods. Getting caught in a wartime situation is obviously never good. Getting caught during BUD/S training can be just as bad, because the instructors make it their mission to drive home the valuable lesson of not getting captured. Anyone who was caught experienced the simulated but still painful realities of POW life. For Jones, being captured was even worse for three reasons. First, Jones was a tadpole officer who'd been through Navy Officer Candidate School. Second, he was a team leader whose job was to set an example for the men who followed him; by getting captured, he'd failed. Third, and worst of all, he was caught cheating on his instructors and his fellow tadpoles.

The Coronado gods who captured Jones noticed a bulge in

---

*Fictional name

his upper clothing and discovered he was wearing a "cheater" (a rubber swim top) under his government-issued shirt that helped keep him somewhat warm in the freezing mudflats. The Coronado gods were enraged. Don't get me wrong—they didn't mind people cheating. After all, if a SEAL ever became a POW, his only chance of survival could be thinking outside the box and breaking the rules. In fact, the mantra was, "If you ain't cheating, you ain't trying." So it wasn't the cheating that aroused the instructors' anger. It was the fact that Jones had allowed himself to get caught doing it, which in a real-world situation would probably have been a life-ending offense at the hands of the enemy.

My swim buddy and I watched from our hiding spot in bushes about fifty feet away. It was about two in the morning, and we were pitch black from head to toe, covered in mud and filth. The whites of our eyes were probably the only hint of our weary existence. No other tadpoles were in sight, but fear permeated the air. We could smell it, even covered head to toe in human waste.

I can still see Jones standing in the black cesspool, crying out for mercy. Like a pride of hungry lions, the Coronado gods verbally gnawed on his weakening heart. The realistic chance of drowning in chest-deep, bone-chilling cold water and liquefied human waste can make a coward of anyone. At about 3:00 a.m., the continuous badgering of the Coronado gods finally succeeded: Jones—a healthy, six-foot-plus, Herculean former Marine—gave up as a tadpole and rang out.

I still wonder whether Jones, had he not been caught, would have graduated and become a proud Navy SEAL. He was a strong tadpole, built like an All-American college fullback, with fast feet for his large, muscular body. He'd probably have made a fine SEAL. However, I also wonder whether he'd ever have felt like a real SEAL, knowing he'd cheated when the rest of BUD/S Class 89 hadn't. Somehow, I don't think so. We felt betrayed by our leader, because this was a test of our raw abilities, and Jones had a secret and artificial advantage. Even though the Coronado gods encouraged being resourceful, how you succeed—the journey—is more important than the fact of your success.

Like Jones, I've made more than my share of mistakes. I imagine you have too. We're all tempted to cut corners. Call it "making bad choices" or "compromising" if that feels better, but in the end, it's still cheating. The good news is I'm forgiven, and so are you. As important as my past may be, it's not nearly as important as the present and the future. Still, in such moments we don't cheat just ourselves; we also cheat friends, family, spouses, and significant others.

But do we ever succeed in cheating God? No. We can cheat fellow man and even the Coronado gods and potentially get away with it, but we can never cheat God, the creator of the universe. Galatians 6:7 tells us, "Don't be misled—you cannot mock the justice of God. You will always harvest what you plant" (NLT). Even if we cheat temporarily, believing we got something by God, can we truly enjoy the journey? It's impossible to trust God and cheat at the same time. One leads us to become more confident as we persevere in life's fiercest storms; the other leads to separation from God.

If you're tempted to cut corners, stop and ask yourself why. Chances are you're robbing your confidence in some aspect of yourself, but ultimately, the temptation to cheat reveals a lack of trust in God. Instead of cheating, go to God, admit your fear or weakness, and ask Him to give you the faith and strength you need to find another way through the situation. The creator of the universe has a way through the predicament and something bigger in mind for you.

Dr. Harold Koenig of Duke University completed an exhaustive analysis of 1,500 medical studies. He concluded that "people who are more religious and pray more have better mental and physical health. . . . In general, they cope with stress better, they experience greater well-being because they have more hope, they're more optimistic, they experience less depression, less anxiety and they commit suicide less often."[7]

Some people who fail to trust God will try to deal with the resulting anxiety through alcohol, smoking, or other addictions. But that doesn't turn out so well. A California pathologist named Thomas Bassler reported an interesting observation: in autopsies of people who died prematurely, two thirds of them revealed a connection to what Bassler called loafer's heart, smoker's lung, or drinker's liver.

How about you? Do you worry when you should be praying? It's a choice we make every day with every thought, not only regarding the big decisions of life but also the many smaller ones. When rumors abounded that Tony Dungy was going to be fired as coach for the Tampa Buccaneers, he was asked about it during a press conference. His reply? "Worrying about my job is not my responsibility; it's God's. My job is to coach."

When you think about a problem over and over in your mind, that's called worry. If you talk to God over and over in your mind, that's called prayer. Why not transform worry into prayer, and allow God to relieve you of your fears?

It's not luck that makes Navy SEALs the most elite combat force in the world; it's hard work and knowing that worry will rob them of the confidence necessary for any mission. They strive for excellence in everything, never quit, and work to build relationships of trust with their team on a daily basis. For Christians, our job is to trust Jesus with every decision, no matter the sacrifice or pain or whatever we're called upon to surrender. It means not running from adversity or giving in to the temptation to cheat, but instead thriving toward it and persevering.

Anyone can cheat, complain, criticize, make excuses, or not put forth the effort necessary to succeed at school, at work, or at home. It's what most fools do. But you are unequivocally wired for greatness, to fulfill a mighty purpose while on this planet. Dwelling on negative possibilities can be as destructive as cancer. It will eventually erode your health and your ability to live abundantly. On the flip side, you can choose to live positively and focus on experiences rather than results.

I once decided to put "enjoy the journey more than the destination" to the test when I asked a dear friend to help me move. It's these kinds of requests that separate true friends from the mere appearance of friendship. Jeff, a busy corporate CEO, responded with something like, "Sure, you can count on me." That Friday, I picked him up, and he was decked out in his finest yet forever-worn moving clothes.

Little did he know that a helicopter was waiting to take us to Atlanta Motor Speedway where we'd drive real NASCAR automobiles around the track like the daredevils we were. Over-the-top competitive men chasing each other while traveling close to 150 mph was a dream fulfilled. Afterward, while driving Jeff home, I pulled over to the side of the road and asked him for his timed lap speed, which had been electronically recorded. Without looking, I took his results and mine, got out of my car, and put them in a nearby trash can. Although Jeff was aghast, wanting to know who had the highest speed, I wanted him to know our day was never about the destination, but the journey.

Of course, not every experience feels positive and fun, but that doesn't mean the experience isn't worthwhile. Every tadpole sucking down Tijuana waste in the bone-chilling mudflats got to check the box if he was in or out. For those who survived, these defining moments of truth did not stop there. Instead, they embraced the moment. They inhaled and exuded strength like oxygen to their lungs.

"If you can't fly," Martin Luther King Jr. once said, "then run. If you can't run, then walk. If you can't walk, then crawl. But whatever you do, you have to keep moving forward."[8]

He didn't realize it, but Dr. King was describing tadpole faith: all-in, all the time.

DARE TO DO THINGS RIGHT

- Step back and see the big picture. In life, the destination matters far less than the journey itself.
- No matter how dire the circumstances, should you be worrying less and praying more?
- Yesterday is already gone, and tomorrow is never guaranteed; so live bravely in the moment of today.

9

PAIN IS WEAKNESS LEAVING THE BODY

Tadpole Faith Is Never Out of the Fight

BY THE MIDPOINT OF HELL Week, running on no sleep for three days (or was it four?), we were like zombies, barely functional as we lurched from one evolution to the next. We were cold and felt the effects of the physical abuse our bodies endured daily. To breathe painlessly—let alone walk without struggle—would have been a miracle. These effects mimicked what could be brought against us by a lethal enemy in wartime.

We swayed on our feet on the golden sand, preparing to run the obstacle course, which sat right on the main highway connecting San Diego to Coronado. Hundreds of cars passed on that road each day. Suddenly, a fellow tadpole named Jimmy broke rank and began walking stoically toward the busy highway. Any man could be robbed of his resolve by the days and nights without sleep, the physical and mental abuse, and the cold Pacific water. All of it had finally gotten to poor Jimmy. He was clearly in a trance, his glazed eyes reflecting the iconic glow of the sunrise.

Each of us had lapsed in and out of a mental coma at one time or another during Hell Week. It was as though we could see and think, but our bodies were in another time zone. Our minds were no longer attached to reality, nor did we want them to be. Pain no longer dominated; it no longer dictated rational or responsive behavior. Yes, we could all identify with Jimmy's temporary insanity.

When Senior Chief Ray saw Jimmy walking toward the highway, his 110-decibel voice popped Jimmy's daydream like a bubble.

"Jimmy! Not even God can help you now!"

It was as if someone above had snapped *His* mighty fingers. Jimmy paused. After what seemed like forever and a day, he turned and walked back to us. His eyes remained glossy; his hypnotic state didn't cease. Still, Jimmy was back with us—physically, if not quite mentally.

Like Jimmy, we can all find ourselves in a daze at times, so overwhelmed by life that we begin wandering away from God and head straight toward trouble. Most times, God doesn't need Senior Chief Ray's thundering voice to get our attention. But whether God shouts or whispers, it's good to know that whenever our faith wavers, we can always count on Him—and our mastermind team—to call us back before we do irreversible damage to ourselves or to others.

The edge that's far more dangerous is where we go beyond the "guardrails" put there to protect us. These guardrails are God's boundaries for our life, as revealed through Scripture. I'm not sure anything is more painful to watch than teenagers, friends, or family members making bad choices and suddenly finding themselves going down a dangerous, slippery slope. When Cain sinned, his guilt disconnected him from God's presence. God said, "You will be a restless wanderer on the earth" (Genesis 4:12, NIV).

God warned us about such people through the apostle Paul: "They wouldn't worship him as God or even give him thanks. And they began to think up foolish ideas of what God was like. As a result, their minds became dark and confused." Now the most important part: "So God abandoned them to do whatever shameful things their hearts desired" (Romans 1:21, 24, NLT).

Nothing has changed. We tend to want to wander toward whatever our flesh desires. If we're not careful, we allow TV shows, movies, music, social media, and worldly influences to kindle desires that dictate our thoughts. Such thoughts become actions, and over time those actions become habits. Then— quicker than a burglar in the night—you may find yourself with Satan on the wrong side of the guardrail, wrapped in darkness. A movie trailer for hell.

On that day in BUD/S Class 89 when Jimmy's mind wandered, there stood Senior Chief Ray to keep him on the proper side of the guardrail. It's what community does. Because of Jimmy's fellow tadpoles and his ironclad resolve, he survived Hell Week, graduated from BUD/S training, and became a Navy SEAL.

I can still hear Senior Chief Ray's fierce motivating words today: "Not even God can help you now!" Sounds just like the enemy, doesn't it? Satan wants us to give up not only on ourselves but also on God. Tadpole faith is fiery and passionate and requires an all-in attitude that locks in on truth. This steadfast faith is available to anyone who decides their faith is more important than whatever fear, temptation, or weakness they are experiencing.

Successful people never give up on goals they believe in. They focus on the finish line throughout the trials. They have locked in no matter the consequences. They don't let anything get in their way, overcoming adversity and seeing possibilities where others do not.

Roy Benavidez was wounded in his right leg, face, and head during a Vietnam rescue helicopter extraction. Still under intense enemy fire, he carried half of the wounded soldiers to a waiting aircraft. Then he returned to retrieve his leader's body but was shot in the abdomen and hit in his back with fragments of a grenade. At the same time, his helicopter crashed, killing the pilot.

With no other option, Benavidez called in another helicopter to attempt a second extraction. On the subsequent extraction attempt, he suffered a broken jaw, was struck by thirty-seven bullets, and received bayonet puncture wounds. He was so seriously wounded and covered in blood that the doctors believed him to be dead and were placing him in a body bag. However, he spat in a doctor's face to prove he was still alive.

Everyone has a "God can't help you now" moment at least once in their life. When yours happens, will it be your moment to spit in the face of the enemy? Will you have the grit to focus on what is excellent and praiseworthy, like your God-given purpose? Tadpole faith teaches us to live from trial to trial throughout the day, never taking a second for granted. Tadpoles are never out of the fight, nor should you be.

Senior Chief Ray's words will ring forever in my ears, but God's promises will echo forever in my heart and soul. Training to be Navy SEAL is painful, but as the Coronado gods say, pain is just weakness leaving the body. This is the mindset that gets many tadpoles through the toughest military training in the world. It also marks the faith of Christ followers, helping them to keep going no matter how dazed, weak, or beaten they are. The good news is, as you become stronger, the pain doesn't hurt as much.

Tony Dungy, in reflecting on the ups and downs of his life and coaching career in his memoir *Quiet Strength,* wrote, "I think people look more closely at our actions in the rough times when the emotions are raw and our guard is down. That's when our true character shows, and we find out if our faith is real. If I'm going to call myself a Christian, I have to honor Jesus in the disappointments too."[9]

Christ followers are never out of the fight, nor do we take God—or our lives—for granted. Tadpole faith teaches us to live from trial to trial throughout the day, never taking a single second or any evolution for granted. Even though, like Roy Benavidez, we may have to spit on a person or two along the way.

God calls all of us to persevere in the midst of the storm, to keep our heads high during the fight, to never surrender. In business or whatever else we strive for in life, we should always perform our very best. James 1:2–4 calls us out far louder than any Coronado god: "When troubles of any kind come your way, consider it as an opportunity for great joy. For you know that when your faith is tested, your endurance has a chance to grow" (NLT). The key phrase here is "opportunity for great joy." That word *opportunity* means it's a choice. And the great joy isn't happiness or even *your* joy necessarily—it's God's joy. This is where faith, trust, and surrender spark our hearts to action.

These moments define not only who we are but *whose* we are.

DARE TO STAY IN THE FIGHT

- Giving up isn't an option. It's not even a real concept. Delete it from your mind.

- Hard times reveal our true ambitions, but above all else, our depth of character. How we respond and who we respond to is everything.

- There are no excuses, only possibilities. Mediocrity is like a lead weight trying to trick you into settling. Don't fall for it.

- No matter how painful the circumstance, God always provides an inversely proportionate equal or greater opportunity.

10

WIDOWS BRING THE BEER

Tadpole Faith Celebrates Always

MANY LIFE LESSONS ARE TAUGHT throughout BUD/S and embraced on the SEAL teams, but one lesson will always stand out for me: SEALs are the best at knowing how to celebrate, no matter how dire the situation. It's an attitude some see as an obsession—though a good one. A culture unto itself, SEALs would not only keep their heads up and keep moving through the pain, they would also sing and smile the entire way. Doing so lessened the misery. It kept their minds in positive motion.

Did you know the word *celebrate* shows up dozens of times throughout the Bible? The Greek word translated as "celebrate" in the New Testament means to be cheerful or happy. It can be used to describe an attitude or behavior.

Although Navy SEALs serving in Vietnam were before my time, I'd heard that whenever a SEAL died, there was a party after the funeral. Not only that, the widows or girlfriends left behind were expected to bring the beer. Before passing judgment, remember that when living with a cloud of debilitating circumstances and even death on a daily basis, you must go to extremes to maintain a forward-thinking attitude. There are no time-outs in war, and that's true for the wives of these daring warriors, who fear a fateful knock on their door in the dawn hours.

Every tadpole needed to acquire this all-in, all the time attitude to graduate from BUD/S. Without it, no tadpole could survive the first day, never mind all the mental and physical punishment and pain to follow. Throughout training, we sang songs while we worked, while we ran to breakfast, while we paddled our boats through six-foot waves, while we locked elbows together when lying in freezing water during Hell Week, while we ran timed four-mile runs in combat boots, and while we were grilled for failing inspections even though we'd been set up well in advance to fail. In fact, pretty much the only time we weren't singing was when we were under water, and if the Coronado gods could have found a way to make us do that without drowning, I'm sure they would have. No matter how much pain we were experiencing, singing those songs established an attitude of survival— of hope that this too shall pass.

According to a Social Indicators Research study of 6.9 million people, Americans are reporting higher levels of depressive symptoms compared to previous decades. High school students report more trouble sleeping, thinking, and remembering, and they say they have episodes of shortness of breath. College students report feeling more overwhelmed. Confirming these findings, the World Happiness Report found Americans to be "significantly" less happy than in previous years.

Explanations abound—stress, more families living apart, less personal time due to demanding technology, and the ever-present violence in media and the movies. On this latter point, Loyola University conducted a brain chemistry study of rats and found that those that watched aggressive behavior in other rats were much more aggressive than rats that didn't observe such behavior.

Times that cause stress and anxiety, those that require focus and grit to get through, should be balanced with times of relaxation and casual fun. Do whatever is necessary to maintain this balance. This character trait of celebrating has singlehandedly delivered success throughout my life, both in the Navy and beyond. It's the glue that keeps me anchored and focused through the tough times.

Guy, my swim buddy, recalls how early in training one of our instructors told us that if we were thinking about ringing out of training, we should do it after rather than in the midst of an evolution. Why? Because even though the next evolution might be just as nasty as the one we were currently in, at least it would be different. And a song or a friendly nudge from a fellow tadpole could be enough to keep us going. That's the sort of glimmer of hope that celebration brings.

The habit of celebrating is essential for anyone seeking a life of abundant joy and success. Whenever the Coronado gods fired their best insults or spine-tingling challenges at us, we had one and only one response: a mighty "Hooyah, yes sir!" followed by smiling and singing all the way. It's an attitude that every employer wants.

We can celebrate also by rejoicing whenever we run into problems and trials, for we know that an all-in, all the time positive attitude will surely help us develop endurance. That endurance develops strength of character while character strengthens our confident hope for good things to come. And this hope will not lead to disappointment.

No matter how tragic the blows of life, we get to choose to rejoice and find the good that God promises in all situations. Romans 8:28 teaches us that God provides good for all those who trust Him in all circumstances. Just don't confuse "good" with "happiness," which is a human construct. I'm convinced that once I chose to find good no matter how miserable the circumstance, God lifted and carried me through those many mind-boggling setbacks in BUD/S. But first I had to decide to celebrate.

Was it easy to celebrate in the mudflats? Absolutely not. But to survive and succeed in BUD/S, tadpoles had to learn to celebrate through all the painful evolutions. I still choose each day to move forward and give my best to find good in every event. I've experienced God's mighty power in all things, which far outweighs the daggers thrown by the world. You can experience this too. If you do, I promise that your heart will persevere through many trials in life, and your faith will shine through any darkness. Your greatest weakness is always God's greatest opportunity.

"That is why we never give up," the apostle Paul teaches us. "Though our bodies are dying, our spirits are being renewed every day" (2 Corinthians 4:16, NLT). Present troubles are small and short-lived. These same troubles produce a glory that vastly outweighs them and will last forever.

Want to know how celebrating affects your body? First, smiling releases neuropeptides that help fight against stress. The body also releases dopamine, endorphins, and serotonin to help you feel better. These neurotransmitters act like natural antidepressants and mood lifters while contributing to an optimal heart rate and blood pressure, keeping your body healthy. Not only does your health increase with a celebratory attitude, you'll also find that you'll be happier overall, content, and more productive.

I cannot think of a better single trait than this for predicting survival through SEAL training—and for thriving throughout the rest of life as well. An all-in, all the time positive attitude is what we desire from our team at work and what we seek in our spouses. This infectious, charismatic, in-demand character trait encourages others and shows appreciation. We electrify the hearts of others as we constantly look for the good in them.

Paul Harvey, one of the great radio talk show broadcasters, once told a story about a teacher who needed help finding a mouse in the classroom. When the teacher asked a blind student to help find it, you can imagine the surprise of the other young students. That student was named Steve Morris, and for the first time, Steve felt special for his excellent hearing ability. Years later, he shared how this single act of appreciation was a new beginning for him. He went on to become famous as the singer and song-writer Stevie Wonder.

You don't have to bring the beer or find a mouse to have joy. You just need to remain focused and have an all-in, all the time positive attitude. Just keep moving forward. Be a champion for others. Keep fighting and never ring out.

Want to think like a Navy SEAL? Learn to celebrate more. Rejoice in all things. Your successes and failures are often a result of what you allow to enter your mind. Think like a champion consistently, and you'll become a champion.

There were hundreds of dark moments in BUD/S where ringing out felt like the only sane thing to do. But I love Habakkuk 3:19, which calls us to remain "surefooted as a deer," especially during life's storms, where negative thoughts tend to multiply like cancer cells. Choose to celebrate others and rejoice in all things, knowing that whatever is negative is merely temporal.

DARE TO CELEBRATE

- Life should be a balance between working hard and playing hard. Have enthusiasm about the colorful, multifaceted life you're cultivating.
- Make laughter an ingredient in every day, even the terrible ones.
- Don't take yourself too seriously, and don't forget to celebrate with others.
- Adversity introduces a man to himself. Be prepared to confidently prove your trust is in God, not yourself.

11

THE OTHER SIDE OF HELL

Tadpole Faith Learns through Adversity

I HAD NO IDEA WHAT day it was, nor did I care. I only knew it was Hell Week.

My body, like my mind, has its limits. We'd endured five and a half days of nonstop pain and misery. After finishing another night of cold-water training, we'd been called to muster near the ocean's edge behind our barracks. My life had already flashed through my mind a dozen times. Was I even alive?

At that point, normal people would have wondered what was next, but we were beyond wondering. We were on automatic. We didn't care. Pain? Misery? Bring it on. Agony had become a way of life. It was home.

Forever faithful, the Coronado gods never let up on their taunting. Toward the end of Hell Week, they were making us carry our IBS boats all the way back to the sand berm where we'd started, but one of the instructors said they were all so disappointed with BUD/S Class 89 that they'd decided we were going to have to stay out an extra day—unless they got one more quitter. If no one volunteered to quit, we were to prepare ourselves for another four-mile run, this time carrying the boat.

The Coronado god who uttered those words eyed the group of solemn yet determined tadpoles with his steely gaze, scrutinizing us for any sign of weakness or capitulation. Not one tadpole blinked, although it may have been the only bodily function we could do without hurting. There were no quitters at that point. Anyone standing there would have died rather than surrendered.

A moment later, as the sun burst over the horizon, something changed about the instructor's posture. It was as though a sudden celebratory mood was in the air, but I knew better. Another trapdoor for the foolish. For us to let our expectations rise was not only unwise but also unsafe.

To my surprise, the Coronado god mumbled four words I did not comprehend for what seemed like an eternity, but seconds later my brain cells caught up with the reality of the moment. Like my fellow sleep-deprived tadpoles, I attempted to connect those seemingly random syllables in my brain. When I did, I realized the announcement was unmistakable, and it would have shocked me, had I been able to feel any emotion.

"Hell Week is secure."

Could it be just another mind game?

Were we about to be served another rat sandwich?

Not that day! Over the berm, they had a cookout going. It was official. Hell Week was over. Those of us still wavering on our feet had survived. Our reward? More pain, punishment, and mind games in the weeks to come, but *first*, a barbecue. And then some rest. A lot of rest.

If I could have walked without chafing pain or talked without a hallucinatory thought, I might have celebrated the moment. With minds that felt bleached of any capacity to hold a thought, our bodies surrendered. After the barbecue, we staggered back to our barracks and collapsed. I slept for two and a half days straight, which only began to put my body back together. It took several weeks to recover completely.

As I recuperated, I reflected on our experience. We'd been

through hell and lived to tell the tale. We hadn't just survived; we'd been taken deep into ourselves, each into his own personal fears, and ordered to jump. All sense of self died that week, left to wither on the windswept beach, to sink to the bottom of the Pacific Ocean, or to rot in the fetid Tijuana mudflats. We were no longer individual tadpoles. Class 89 was now one body, one mind, a single community that had survived Hell Week. Our only goal was to enter phase two of BUD/S and to help our fellow tadpoles do the same. To put one foot in front of the other. To breathe in and breathe out. To conquer. To endure.

I realized the purpose of Hell Week was not just to break us down or to weed out the weaklings but also to lay a new foundation for everything to come. It was designed to give us a stark realization of our limitations as individuals and to emphasize our need for our swim buddies and for each other. In a word, to humble us. We encouraged each other when our bodies said, "No more." We carried each other, and we did it with enthusiasm. We were never lazy, always alert, and always forward-thinking.

Tadpoles after Hell Week are known for their superior confidence. When the Coronado gods threw personal insults at us, daring us to drop out, we remained steadfast. Being a team and loving each other prepared us for the battlefields to come. Looking out for our teammates was as instinctive as breathing. We knew that if we listened to the Coronado gods' orders, obeyed them to the best of our ability, and helped our fellow tadpoles do the same, there was nothing we couldn't accomplish. In war, caring for each other is not only expected but demanded; by now it was second nature.

Since Hell Week, I've endured many other experiences that, although not as physically excruciating, have brought me to a similar realization of my limitations as an individual. I've been forced to depend immeasurably more on God's voice. Emptied of myself in such moments, I've become teachable and eager to learn what I've been missing and how to apply it to any situation.

This means spending quality time in God's Word. I often prayed, but I came to realize this had largely been me talking *to* God. Eventually, I learned the importance of how *God speaks to us* through the Scriptures. Whenever my faith wanders, it almost always parallels a failure to spend time listening to what God has to say.

Not everyone is called to become a Navy SEAL, but every child of God is called to be bold and courageous. As Winston Churchill reportedly said, "If you're going through hell, keep going." Hell Week is not to be feared; it's to be embraced, knowing that the person who emerges on the other side will be stronger, humbler, and better equipped to help the entire team reach its objectives.

During that week the bell rang loud and often as the helmets lined up beneath it. I saw miracles come and go. At the beginning of Hell Week, we had eighty tadpoles. Five and a half days later, we had around thirty. But if we thought things were about to get easier, we were dead wrong. We were quickly introduced to another kind of hell—a kind I didn't think possible.

DARE TO BE TEACHABLE IN CHALLENGING TIMES

- Even the cushiest life is a series of Hell Week challenges, but you are called to succeed. Go beyond the horizon every day without exception.
- Strive to be wise. Wisdom trumps knowledge—only God gives wisdom.
- Be grateful for challenges, because character and skill don't come from doing easy things. The easy life is easy but never worth following.

12

DON'T BECOME SHARK BAIT

*Tadpole Faith Embraces Fear Instead of
Running Away from It*

FOR PHASE TWO, WE SPENT twenty-one days on San Clemente Island, an isolated refuge fifty miles off the California coast. Although at the beginning of our time on San Clemente, we learned we weren't quite as isolated as we'd thought. A team of hunters had landed on the island at around the same time to help curb the feral goat population, so for a brief time, we found ourselves dodging real bullets.

A highlight of our time on the island was a two-mile night swim. As usual, the swimming conditions were far from ideal—the waters surrounding the island were known as a fertile feeding ground for great white sharks. Being from the hills of Georgia, I did not have an affinity for those lovely creatures. Right before the night swim, the Coronado gods forced us to watch filmstrips about the dangers of sharks, their ability to rip apart human flesh and bones, and their insatiable appetite for blood—especially tadpole blood. They showed us photos of shark-attack victims, most of whom had died from their wounds. I'd heard that the Coronado gods were known to throw animal blood on tadpoles right before the swim—not that we needed to be made any more appetizing. But the instructors didn't stop there. They also warned us about barracudas, coral fish, rock snakes, and every other denizen of the deep that was waiting out there to devour us. All this was horrific news for BUD/S Class 89's slowest swimmer (me) and his swim buddy, Guy.

As I suited up, I said my final prayers. I knew how important it was to let my faith be bigger than my greatest fear, but it still felt as if dinner had been my last meal. It was closing in on midnight, and the water was a frigid 55°F. With my heart pounding and skipping beats, we spat into our masks and washed them out with water to prevent them from fogging up. Even at night, we liked to see where we were going. All I could see was the light of the moon reflecting off the water. I imagined the lethal shapes cruising in the dark below. Guy was already planning his getaway once the sharks spotted the slowest member of the pack, and I didn't blame him.

However, something about the swim that night was different. Really different. I can't say exactly why, but Guy and I felt a burst of energy, beginning with our first stroke. Probably because we found ourselves surrounded immediately by all the creatures of the ocean—although we only saw kelp, our bodies were on high alert. Fear has a way of giving you that extra push. For the first time, other team members were not passing us, as they had during all our previous swims. I was convinced the sharks had found other prey.

We glided, stroke by stroke, as though we were swimming for Olympic gold. I couldn't believe it. If only Master Chief Saunders could have seen me. As we approached the finish point, my sense of amazement grew. As far as I knew, all my limbs were still attached. And for the first time, Guy and I finished closer to the front of the pack than the rear!

Our success did not go unnoticed by the Coronado gods, who naturally assumed our previous performances were due to not trying hard enough. They punished us accordingly by yelling at us, calling us slackers, and demanding we do a hundred push-ups on the spot. The easiest hundred push-ups I ever had the pleasure of pumping out!

Punishment aside, isn't it amazing what a little fear can do if channeled properly? More times than not, fear is a mind game, a choice. Fear doesn't have to be the enemy. It can and should be your ally. It can keep you safe, like telling you to avoid the path of an angry pitbull or to not touch a red-hot stove. It can also be a daring invitation for something more. I believe we all have the God-given ability to channel fear into positive energy. This means processing fear and anxiety to our advantage.

Michael Thornton, a Medal of Honor winner and one of my Coronado gods, once held off fifty or so North Vietnamese along with two other buddies. After five hours of this, he was told that one of his buddies had been shot. He made a moment-of-truth decision to run back about 400 yards and pick up his nearly dead teammate while killing several more North Vietnamese in defense. I dare say his adrenaline flow ignited his reaction time to take out the enemy in nanoseconds while running at a speed that Usain Bolt would envy—I cannot imagine Thornton casually walking during a firefight with fifty soldiers. He then rushed back to the sea, where he and his companions had come from, and swam almost two hours while towing his wounded teammate before being picked up.

Sometimes fear gets a bad rap. Think about it.

According to Penn State kinesiologist Vladimir Zatsiorsky, we use only about sixty-five percent of our natural muscle strength under normal conditions. When the body is under stress or danger, the brain releases powerful analgesics called endocannabinoids and opioids that override the pain while performing daring tasks. Then our brain releases neurotransmitters called norepinephrine—commonly referred to as adrenaline. In fact, this adrenaline is so desired by some performers that they've learned how to induce fear in order to perform at their peak.

Make fear your ally. Decide how you will respond to it. Will you allow it to paralyze you or will you channel it to give you the extra push with a quicker mind? For professional performers and SEALs, it's often a chosen, natural way to increase muscle strength, ignore pain, and enable maximum performance, all without taking a pill.

Fearful situations are unavoidable. What's important is not the fear itself but how we respond to it. Like Navy SEALs, Christ followers can embrace fear, learn from it, and regard it as nothing more than a growing pain. We all decide how we deal with fear. Many deny it. Some run from it. The wise become wiser because of it. But it's always a choice. We're not to run *away* from fear but *toward* it. To a Navy SEAL, there are no such things as problems, only opportunities. The same is true for Christians. God doesn't keep us from our fears but instead offers us the capacity to meet those fears—and overcome them. Without such fears, we wouldn't grow or experience courage.

During parachute jumps, we'd always have two parachutes: the main canopy strapped tightly to our back and a much smaller one on our front, a reserve in case the primary chute did not deploy. In the teams, this little life-saving reserve was nicknamed "Little Jesus." I now see how I chose to respond to fear as another "Little Jesus." It deploys whenever the ropes are tightened or during my own moments of truth.

May "Little Jesus" deploy whenever you feel the instant fear of rejection or failure or hear painful words like, "You need to find a new job somewhere else," or even "I'm afraid it's terminal." You may have no idea what horrors are lurking beneath the surface of the future; however, the sure way to overcome those leviathans is not to focus on them but to keep your eyes fixed on the goal and keep moving forward, stroke by stroke, until you emerge beyond the monster's reach.

Even if you have to do 100 push-ups afterward, you'll be happy for the opportunity to do so.

DARE TO USE YOUR FEAR

- Without fear, there would be no courage. It's instinctive. Use it to your advantage.

- Preparation, courageous faith, and trusting God are the antidotes to fear.

- Courageous people know how to use fear and anxiety to their advantage. Being afraid is like being energized: your muscles are stronger when you feel fear. You can sharpen this feeling.

13

FIRE IN THE HOLE

Tadpole Faith Pays Attention

PHASE TWO OF BUD/S TRAINING was nine weeks long, and it was all about land warfare. We learned navigation, small-unit land warfare tactics, patrolling techniques, rappelling, and working with C-4, a powerful plastic explosive. One of the best parts of being a tadpole was the opportunity to play with things that went *boom!* Being on San Clemente Island allowed us to learn the business of war without waking up the neighbors—working with guns, explosives, you name it, we lived out every boy's dream. Getting paid to blow up stuff is the pinnacle of unadulterated thrills. However, just because it was fun didn't mean we took it lightly. Safety was always uppermost in our minds.

Before setting off explosives, it was not only customary but also required for the igniter to yell, "Fire in the hole!" seconds before detonation, so everyone else had time to take cover. Thanks to such precautions, we didn't have a single accident during our explosives training. As long as we practiced similar safety procedures when working as Navy Special Warfare operators on real missions, that safety record would hopefully continue.

The problem with warnings is that the more often we hear them, the less we tend to heed them. For example, if you've done any amount of flying, you've had countless experiences of hearing flight attendants tell you where the exits are located, how to use your seat belt, and what to do in case of an emergency water landing. You could probably recite the procedures in your sleep.

Or could you?

If you're a frequent flyer like me, it's more likely that as soon as the flight attendants step up to make their presentation, you bury your nose in the pages of a book or magazine or put your earbuds in to listen to your favorite music or audiobook. You probably haven't paid close attention to the safety presentation in years. Considering how planes have changed over time, in the event of an actual emergency, how prepared would you be?

Throughout life, we don't just hear external warnings; we hear many internal warnings as well. "Don't take a second look at her." "Put it back; it doesn't belong to you." "Don't visit that website." Such warnings come from our conscience, the part of us that God uses to sound the alarm when we're on the verge of doing something that could harm us or others. The problem is, the more times we hear such warnings and don't suffer the consequences immediately, the easier it is to ignore them. Soon we're going through life like a frequent flyer, ignoring the "safety presentation" in our mind, thinking all that preparation is a waste of time—until disaster strikes. Then we suddenly find ourselves in the midst of a potentially catastrophic situation for which we're entirely unprepared. We've been tested, and we've failed.

After my days in the Navy, I learned the value of heeding such warnings as an entrepreneur. I experienced a lot of success—to the point that a major company made an offer to buy my business. After intense negotiations, we agreed to a deal, and the company's vice president and corporate attorney flew all the way from the West Coast to my home in Atlanta to sign the contract and personally deliver a nice fat check that required both hands to count the digits.

The VP arrived first and was one of the nicest, most down-to-earth Ivy League intellectuals you'll ever meet. Everything was going well. It was a "Where do I sign?" kind of moment.

Then the corporate attorney showed up. He was a little more formal and apparently had left all his manners in California. That was understandable; he was a man on a mission. After I greeted him at our front door, I walked him and the VP downstairs to my home office. After some brief conversation, I asked the attorney for a few minutes so I could review a couple of minor contract clarifications with him. It was nothing that would have halted the deal, so the attorney's response surprised me.

"Listen, if you're not ready to sign this contract right now, I can get back on my plane and be home this time tomorrow."

I was stunned.

A negative vibe hovered in my office for a few brief moments. Was it a warning? No doubt the attorney thought there was no way I would walk away from a check for millions. Yet almost instantly I heard that internal voice as though the Holy Spirit showed up. I relayed the words it seemed to whisper to me carefully to the attorney: "Enjoy your trip home."

He was shocked, as though time had been frozen.

Without hesitation I stood and ushered him to my front door.

Was the company's offer a great deal for me financially? Absolutely. But by then I'd learned not to second-guess God's warnings, His gentle whispers of discernment. No matter the size of my bank account, it didn't trump my peace, joy, and happiness. God's warnings are rarely delivered in a dramatic "Fire in the hole!" fashion. More often they're a faint but distinctive feeling. But the consequences of ignoring them are just as real.

The irony of the situation is that in the following months, my business increased by almost a third, following the unanticipated acquisition of a huge new client.

These warnings guide us in all areas of our lives. A dear friend once tearfully confessed his addiction to porn while on a men's Christian retreat at a lakeside location. He followed the Holy

Spirit's warnings by taking his laptop, the source of his addiction, and tossing it into the lake. He decided that his wife, family, and relationship with God were more important.

Your successes and failures are often determined by what you allow to enter your mind. Think like a champion, and you'll be a champion; think like a fool, and you'll become one. The good news is that it's a choice. No human can think two thoughts simultaneously, meaning, you *choose*.

For me, whenever harmful or impure thoughts from the enemy attack, I fight back by opening God's Word. Or I exercise, take a walk, pray, call up a friend, or read a worthwhile book. The key is having confidence in your ability to make wise decisions. Confidence is not a gift; it's earned. It requires fortitude, daring, hard work, and the innate wisdom of seeing the other side of real-life storms. Wisdom means seeing life from God's perspective.

Whether the warnings come externally or internally, get in the habit of paying attention to them. You may think you can safely ignore the warning because it's only a drill, or you're not in the midst of a crisis, or you don't see anything bad coming. Little do you realize that ignoring the warning could be the very thing that induces the catastrophe from which God has been trying to protect you all along, preventing you from benefiting from the opportunity that's right around the corner.

Listening to God means more than just listening in the moment. It also means reading and meditating on the Scriptures consistently so that when such moments arise, God's Word is already planted in your mind, ready to raise its voice when needed.

Yes, I walked away from millions that day. Not only did it feel great to have the moral strength and integrity to do so, but I also enjoyed looking at my face in the mirror the following morning. And I'm pretty sure God did too.

DARE TO LISTEN CAREFULLY AND CONSCIOUSLY

- We talk to God through prayer, and He speaks to us through His Word. All strong relationships require two-way communication. Are you talking? Are you listening?

- Avoid worldly trapdoors; listen to the warnings that come from the Holy Spirit and then take precautionary measures.

- Everyone wants dessert first, but life doesn't work that way. Getting a thumbs-up from God is the endgame, and that doesn't come until later.

- Wisdom, skill, fortitude, work ethic . . . all of these things are built grain by grain. That's why these traits are so rare today.

14

LIVING IN AN APPROVAL-ADDICTED WORLD

Tadpole Faith Is Like a Sociopath—in a Good Way

ANOTHER HIGHLIGHT ON SAN CLEMENTE Island was an evolution that involved being tied to the side of a high-speed boat to avoid detection by the enemy, getting dropped off at sea, then swimming toward shore and laying a "det" field (detonation field). We would lay out a half-mile of detonation cord attached to C-4 explosive and blow up concrete obstacles, like those left over from World War II that were designed to sink amphibious boats if they came too close to shore. The exercise required all twenty or so tadpoles to work in concert, and it was all done underwater with snorkels.

Having C-4 strapped to your body while working underwater as a team requires perfection. There was no margin for error. Even apart from a deep-sea environment, placing C-4 is an art form. Everyone worked together, each man doing his part quickly, efficiently, and silently. We attached it to the obstacle while the detonation cord was connected to the blast caps, which joined one C-4 charge to the next. Our work was like a well-choreographed underwater dance.

Once the finely woven spider web of destruction was laid, we began our swim back out to sea to be picked up by a high-speed boat. We swam quickly, since the det field we'd just laid was live and about to light up the sky. Along the way, I noticed a dead shark trapped in a fishing net in about fourteen feet of water. I recognized it as my chance to become a BUD/S legend as the brave, tough tadpole who caught a shark with his bare hands (and, of course, his K-bar knife). I could already see the photo: me standing on the beach holding up a four-foot shark impaled on my knife. Most importantly, I would be able to tell the story of how I'd wrestled and killed the shark with my bare hands. Such a brave soul! No more being known as the "back in the hills" Georgia boy who swam like a rock. Yes, in that moment I was willing to deceive my peers if it meant basking in the glow of their admiration.

Without hesitation, I pulled out my K-bar; took a long, deep breath; and down I went. Knowing I had only seconds to cut the shark free before I'd have to return to the surface, I worked quickly. But as I grabbed the shark, I realized I'd made a potentially fatal error. The shark wasn't dead! Did I mention it was also tremendously quicker than I was? Thankfully, this desperate but angry shark was somewhat restrained by the net, which gave me just enough time to spike up out of the water like a torpedo!

As quickly as I'd begun to imagine being on the island's highlight reel as the brave soul who'd killed a shark with his bare hands, my hopes plummeted. But for the moment, I was just happy my error hadn't cost me a limb—or worse.

Have you ever literally risked your life to get attention and admiration from others? Isn't it interesting the ridiculous lengths to which we're willing to go to get noticed? I've done that more times than I care to admit, but BUD/S training had a way of beating that tendency out of us. Most tadpoles abided by the same rule of the road: stay in the middle of the pack. On runs and swims, we tried to avoid being noticed by the instructors for being too close to the front or, worse, too far toward the back. Making either mistake would put us on the Coronado gods' radar and expose us to their never-ending wrath.

In real life, however—especially in our approval-addicted world—it seems as if everyone wants to be recognized, to receive positive attention from other people. As if getting God's attention isn't enough. Of course, every human has a need for affection and acceptance. However, if we're not careful, we can become so self-focused that we forget to pursue our God-given mission here on earth.

What makes a person successful? I've researched dozens of articles and other sources to explore the world's answers to this question. These authors mentioned the key traits of all successful people, such as how to walk into a room and own it, how to be a charismatic leader, and so on. Being a "strong communicator" is often ranked second. As Theodore Roosevelt said, "The royal road to a person's heart is to talk about the things he or she treasures most." Interestingly, "loving big" was ranked as the most popular trait. The most successful people were seen as being others-focused, always grateful, personable, and tolerant, always striving to build positive relationships.

Zig Ziglar observed that as you do more for others, you can't help but help yourself. *The Atlantic* magazine gave a great example of this in a story about a nonprofit organization, Experience Corps, that recruited volunteer academic tutors. The tutors, who were retired, helped disadvantaged kindergarten and early elementary students in nineteen cities, with the goal of improving their academic performance. The results were positive for the students. But the kicker was the reported impact on the aging tutors: their depression rates fell; their physical mobility, stamina, and flexibility increased; and their mental functioning and memory was sharpened.

We're all tempted to bring glory to ourselves, just as I was that day with the shark. I learned, however, that serving my team and my country rather than myself comes with its own rewards.

You'll rarely meet a Navy SEAL who exalts himself, for his confidence is already complete from his accomplishments.

These words are the ethos of the Navy SEAL Foundation: "My loyalty to country and team is beyond reproach. I humbly serve as a guardian to my fellow Americans, always ready to defend those who are unable to defend themselves. I do not advertise the nature of my work, nor seek recognition for my actions." If I'd been faithfully serving my team and less concerned about my adoration after laying the live det field that day, I'd have been a lot less motivated to wrestle with a shark. One thing is certain, I've learned to forever embrace Philippians 2:3: "Don't be selfish; don't try to impress others. Be humble, thinking of others as better than yourselves" (NLT).

DARE TO IGNORE THE APPROVAL OF OTHERS

- Our society is too focused on surface perceptions, and we place too much attention on the opinions of others. Not every perspective is worthy of your time.
- As you grow, be prepared to be alone without being lonely. Be comfortable going against the grain.
- Avoid Satan's slow-dying water torture strategies of comparing. Should we spend less time focusing on others and ourselves in the mirror and more time looking to God? Only His approval has long-term benefits.

15

THE NITROGEN NARCOSIS THAT KILLS

Tadpole Faith Doesn't Hide Flaws; It Embraces Them

ONCE PHASE TWO WAS IN our rearview mirror, I thought the hard part was over and it would be all downhill from there. Boy, was I wrong. Phase three of BUD/S training concentrated on perfecting our diving skills. We learned everything there was to know about underwater combat and diving physiology. In the classroom and in the pool, they taught us what could happen if we made a mistake while underwater, how to respond if our equipment failed or was damaged, and how to fix it, if possible.

To prepare us for possible combat and disaster scenarios, we were placed in situations that tested our ability to perform under extreme circumstances. That's where the pool harassment drills came into play. During such exercises, our instructors attacked us underwater, tearing off our flippers, ripping our regulators out of our mouths, or tearing off and discarding our masks. Other times they shut off our air behind our backs, tied our regulator hoses in knots, or unscrewed them and tossed them aside. Sometimes two instructors would attack at once, the first one punching the diver in the stomach while the other one messed with the diver's equipment. To pass the exercise, we had to find our equipment and get it functioning properly again before breaching the pool's surface. If we came up before we had our equipment functioning, we had to do it again. If we failed one too many times or had performance failures, we were out.

One of the most dangerous aspects of combat diving is returning to the surface without air if your regulator is damaged. If not trained properly, divers can become severely injured or even die if they don't know how to surface properly. When breathing from a tank, a diver is breathing compressed air, which has the same pressure the water is exerting. The longer a diver is underwater, the more nitrogen is released into the body. Coming back to the surface too quickly can produce the same effect on your blood as unscrewing the lid from a soda bottle that's been shaken up: it can explode. In the body, this effect is produced by the buildup of nitrogen and other gasses in the blood. Not only is it extremely painful but it also can cause the limbs to distort and bend, hence the nickname "the bends." And it can be fatal.

Nitrogen narcosis is another condition that can occur because of a buildup of nitrogen in the blood. Divers commonly call this condition "rapture of the deep." It starts to become apparent at a depth of 100 feet and can be deadly at 300 feet. It can impair nerve impulses and cause disorientation and loss of physical and mental dexterity, resulting in slower reaction times and diminished reasoning ability. It produces an effect much like being drunk or high on drugs.

Wallowing in the depths of sin and addiction can have consequences as lethal as staying too deep underwater for too long. However, just like a diver transitioning out of deep water, trying to exit such an unhealthy lifestyle too abruptly, or without the proper assistance or equipment in place, can be deadly.

If you find yourself stuck at the bottom of the pool with your gear torn off and Satan's minions harassing you, first of all, don't panic. Second, determine what you'll need to help you get back to the surface, then get all the proper pieces in place. Finally, don't expect change to happen overnight. Pace your journey back out of the depths so that the transition to the surface doesn't inadvertently send you back down into deeper trouble than you were in before.

During events like divorce, death of a loved one, addictions, or any hurtful experience, Satan preys on your feelings, spreading anger, sadness, despair, or guilt throughout your mind and body. If you're not totally focused on Christ, such negative feelings can become as deadly as an ice pick. By remaining in God's Word and consistent prayer, you'll gain wisdom, and your faith will expand your heart. Then you'll be better equipped to resist the temptation to ring the bell or to buy into the clever but painful lies from Satan's lips.

No matter how many thorns Satan gouges into my heart, the following words from Jeremiah 17:7–8 always provide protection: "Blessed is the man who trusts in the LORD, whose trust is the LORD. He is like a tree planted by water, that sends out its roots by the stream and does not fear when heat comes" (ESV).

No SEAL got through BUD/S without being bold, brave, and courageous. Above all, he never gave up. However, as tough as BUD/S is, life can be exponentially tougher. Did you know that the worst of ocean storms, hurricanes, and typhoons are never felt below twenty-five feet in the ocean? Down there you'll find total calm, no matter the storm. There's also one place where you can find similar peace and joy amid the storms of life: in oneness with the creator of heaven and earth.

I've weathered some of life's worst storms, including a battle with cancer. I've experienced the pangs of hunger as a young man while starting a new business—and worse by far, the death of a son. Emotional needle pricks of missing him never waver.

Don't give in to the thorn in your flesh. Instead, become a thorn in Satan's flesh. Disrupt his plans to overthrow your life and God's kingdom. Our troubles should not erode our faith but instead launch our faith to new levels.

Tadpoles who go on to become SEALs don't panic or run from their pain, fears, or anxieties; they run *toward* them. They know such flaws complete their story, and they grow from them. They believe there are no problems in life, only opportunities.

One thing is for certain, *we* get to choose.

DARE TO RISE STEADILY OUT OF TRYING TIMES

- Hardships, trials, or perceived failures are the secret ingredients for realizing God's plan for you.
- Tribulations are setups, not setbacks. They are an obstacle course to beat.
- Acknowledge the bigger plan that you can't see.

16

DROP AND GIVE ME FIFTY

Tadpole Faith Rarely Argues, and It Never Criticizes

In addition to work in the pool, phase three of BUD/S was dedicated to ocean dives, often twice a day. As tadpoles, we became full-time divers. We lived in cold water day and night, like it was our second home.

During the diving phase, the Coronado gods began to reveal a bit of their human side to us. One day when the sun was shining—the perfect time for an ocean dive—twenty tadpoles and several instructors were on a small PT boat returning from a dive somewhere in the Pacific. We were all enjoying the ride. The stars aligned that day, and I did the unusual. Not only did I tell a joke but it was funny—funny enough that even Senior Chief Ray worked up a smile. Then, laughing, he told me to drop and give him fifty. Just because he could.

Without a blink, I got down with two eighty-pound diving tanks on my back and pumped out fifty push-ups for him, smiling the entire time. Did I question his sanity? No. Did I hesitate? Absolutely not. Whenever a Coronado god said "jump," our goal was to leap as high as we could, smiling all the while no matter the pain. We never asked for details no matter how insane the command—and some of the commands were maniacal!

My good buddy Doug Young (BUD/S Class 89 honor recruit) served on the teams for twenty years and eventually became a BUD/S instructor. He often gave tadpoles the following advice on getting through the program: "This is the secret: you wake up early in the morning, go to your locker, unscrew your head, and place it on the locker shelf. Then shut the locker and go about your day. In the evening, after the last BUD/S evolution, go back to your locker, open it, pick up your head, and screw it back on." That about summed things up.

Such unquestioning submission to the Coronado gods not only helped me survive BUD/S training but also proved an ideal training ground for marriage. I tend to want to do things *my* way. I like to refer to it as wisdom, but more often than not it cashes out as selfishness.

I wonder what would happen to all marriages if husbands and wives placed each other's desires before their own and submitted in this fashion. When I say "submit," I don't mean become a doormat. I mean to place your spouse's needs and interests before your own. That means becoming a stronger person by being a better listener and following Jesus' example in how He submitted to His Father. It means living a life of action-oriented love. It also means faithfully imitating God. I don't believe there's a single long-term joyful relationship that doesn't involve some form of continued submission. I realize this idea goes against the grain of our flesh, which always seeks to fulfill our selfish desires; but it goes perfectly *with* the grain of God's kingdom.

Submission is difficult, especially if, like me, you tend to think you're right most of the time. But even in situations where you know you're right, setting that aside and attuning yourself to your partner's needs will go a long way toward establishing a relationship of trust.

On another level, I've found that criticizing is never time well spent. If you are only focused on criticizing the other person, both parties walk away feeling they're still right. The argument was futile, so why bother? I've also found that criticism instinctively breeds resentment, no matter how right you may be. Truth be told, any fool can criticize others. Noted endocrinologist Hans Selye once said, "As much as we thirst for approval, we dread condemnation." The people I admire most have the uncanny ability to listen and relate to others, no matter how dire their own circumstances.

So the next time someone you love asks you to drop and give them fifty, even if the command seems out of line, don't protest. Just smile and do as you're told. You might be surprised at the result!

DARE TO SUBMIT

- Don't be a doormat, but be willing to put the needs of others first whenever appropriate. Submission is important in every relationship, especially your relationship with God.
- Find the best in others. Be a thoughtful listener, and give every person dignity and respect in every interaction. Everyone belongs in this world and has a right to speak.
- You'll be amazed at how much you get by always giving more.

17

IT'S HARD TO BREATHE
WITHOUT OXYGEN

*Tadpole Faith Surrenders the Pen and Lets God Write
the Story*

IN THE THIRD PHASE OF BUD/S, we did many night dives in murky San Diego Bay. A typical evolution involved attaching fake bombs to the hull of a Navy ship. To guide us through the water, which offered close to zero visibility even during the daytime, we used compass boards. A compass board is not a high-tech device. It is a board with a compass attached dead center with handles on both sides, allowing the lead diver to monitor his direction while kicking his fins full steam ahead toward the target. Keeping an eye on the compass was vital because a one- or two-degree deviation in either direction for a minute or two could put the diver and his swim buddy way off course over a two-mile swim. To avoid that, the lead diver would plant his mask right on top of the compass while his swim buddy kept his eye out for enemy forces—in our case, sharks and other hazards of the deep.

This is the posture we need to adopt as we find our way through life—except, instead of the compass board, we must keep our eyes fixed on God's Word. If we do, we'll remain on course.

The minute we take our eyes off God's Word, we begin to drift away from the truth, joy, love, and peace God wants for us.

Staying focused on the Word requires precision as well as discipline. It's always tempting to lift your head and look around, especially when temptations come your way. You may worry that you might be missing out on something, or fear what might be lurking out there in the darkness. However, if you remember that your swim buddy, Jesus, is always with you and watching out for you, it's far easier to keep your head down and your eyes on the compass.

I often get lazy and either take my eyes off the compass of God's Word or toss the compass away and attempt to find my way on my own. Either way, Satan's clutching grasp is waiting for me—just as it waits for you. There's no escape. The warning in Proverbs 25:28 holds nothing back: "A man without self-control is like a city broken into and left without walls" (ESV).

Galatians 5:22–23 lists the nine fruit of the Spirit. The least talked about virtue is self-control. Each fruit of the Spirit is important, but can you imagine the relationships that would be healed if everyone exercised biblical self-control? How many jail cells would be empty today? How many marriages and friendships would remain intact?

God desires your heart, your faith, and your surrender—an intimate relationship with you—these will provide you with lasting joy. "The greatness of anyone's power," said William Booth, founder of the Salvation Army, "is the measure of their surrender."

To survive BUD/S, I had to learn how to surrender. If I hadn't surrendered to the Coronado gods and become a member of a team with my fellow tadpoles, the bell would have been rung for me. Life is no different. God's greatest desire is for us to experience joy, happiness, and peace; but to have all this from the one who created us, we must surrender to Him. I mean totally surrender, not holding anything back. The joy we experience is directly proportional to the measure we surrender to God. My pastor,

Louie Giglio, expresses it this way: "Surrender the pen, and let God write your story." Simple words, but they're not always easy to follow.

How do we surrender? Hebrews 12:1 says, "Let us strip off every weight that slows us down, especially the sin that so easily trips us up. And let us run with endurance the race God has set before us" (NLT).

I'm thankful that I never dropped the compass board on any dive. If I had, no doubt I would have found myself lost in dark, murky waters with no air left in my tanks. *The Word is like oxygen to our lungs.*

DARE TO SURRENDER

- Know that it is okay not to be in control.
- The joy we experience is often directly proportional to the measure we surrender to God's Word. The Word is like oxygen to the lungs of all those who want lasting joy.
- God speaks in quiet, meaningful whispers, not in heavy-handed thunderbolts. If you listen, He'll breathe into you all the guidance you'll ever need.

18

WHO PACKED YOUR PARACHUTE?

Tadpole Faith Leaps with Confidence

FOR THE FEW WHO MAKE it through BUD/S, life will never be the same. Class 89 began with a couple of hundred hopefuls. On graduation day, we had only twenty of those original tadpoles left. These graduates would likely never know the word *impossible* for the rest of their living days on earth. Perfection would no longer be the exception but the rule. And for their spouses, living with a SEAL would require equal heroism.

The only thing left before we became official SEALs was jump school in New Jersey. After all we'd been through, jumping out of an airplane at 5,000 feet was nothing. The truth is, jump school felt like a graduation party that lasted several days and nights. We did a lot of celebrating, chest pounding, and backslapping. In fact, during our first jump, most of us were exhausted from partying it up the night before. But when the jumpmaster gave the thumbs-up sign to line up and jump out, we were sober in an instant.

You never forget your first time leaping out of an airplane. At that moment, I wished only one thing: that I'd paid more attention in the parachute-packing class the day before since we all packed our own parachutes for the jump. With no time to recheck it, all I could do was say a quick prayer, hope for the best, and abandon myself to gravity.

You go through several phases of mental stimulation when jumping out of a plane. It's a huge adrenaline rush and is not for the weak of heart. As your body races toward the ground, the wind hammers at your face, pushing back your skin. Once your parachute deploys, everything changes again. A sudden jerk, a rush up, and then silence. Free-floating. You never tire of the panoramic view. When you see things from an eagle's perspective, you realize you're so much smaller than you thought you were. During my first jump, I had plenty of time on the way down to reflect on the fact that underestimating the jump school phase of training could have easily cost me my life. Thankfully, some of the parachute-packing instructions had sunk in despite the amount of celebration. Rather than plunging to my death, after a brief free fall, I floated safely to the ground.

Another parachute jump danger worth mentioning is "ground rush," the illusion that the ground is rushing up to meet you. This occurs when the jumper locks eyes on the ground right before landing, increasing the possibility of temporary shock. At that point, a proper landing is no longer possible.

Life is the same, isn't it? In the midst of adversity, we tend to focus on the problems rushing toward us. It's so easy to allow the enemy to paralyze us with anxiety and fear when our attention should remain focused on the creator of the universe instead. As Christ followers, we should keep our eyes locked on Jesus with God's all-powerful confidence.

Remember, storms of life are unavoidable; it's how we respond to them that matters. You'll likely find that almost every SEAL and every successful leader of any thriving company or organization will be an expert at responding to adverse situations. I believe this is what God has called every Christ follower to be as well. David gives us a powerful faithful warrior's prayer: "The Lord is my light and my salvation—so why should I be afraid? The

LORD is my fortress, protecting me from danger, so why should I tremble? When evil people come to devour me, when my enemies and foes attack me, they will stumble and fall. Though a mighty army surrounds me, my heart will not be afraid. Even if I am attacked, I will remain confident" (Psalm 27:1–3, NLT).

This kind of courage is a whole lot easier if we're convinced that our parachutes are packed properly *before* we jump out of the plane. How do we prepare to confront Satan's tradecraft of fear and anxiety? By steadfastly reading Scripture, praying, meditating, and staying in close fellowship with other believers. Then when God, the jumpmaster, orders you out, you can step into the empty air with the confidence that you will land safely and enjoy the view on the way.

DARE TO LEAP WHEN TOLD

- Carrying guilt, worries and troubles proves we're not truly trusting God. Maintain your faith through prayer and reading Scripture so you are prepared when dark times challenge you—and they will.

- Keep your focus on God and not the problems rushing to meet you.

- Your greatest fear is always God's greatest opportunity.

19

BUCK-NAKED CINDERELLA MEN

Tadpole Faith Sometimes Needs Grace

Days after Hell Week, a tadpole can be noticed a mile away by the way he walks, due to blistering rashes, and the sleepless glare in his eyes. After graduation, a tadpole is nothing less than a bona fide Spartan.

Every tadpole that successfully completes BUD/S training and jump school is sent to a designated UDT/SEAL team: half go to the East Coast in Little Creek, Virginia, and the rest head back to Coronado. There were only five teams then, and now there are ten. However, the biggest change is that Navy SEALs are no longer America's greatest secret.

I was assigned to an East Coast team, and one of my first deployments was to the Mediterranean. A perk of being deployed there was getting to take our leaves in some of the most desirable vacation spots in the world, including the beautiful city of Marseille in the south of France. On one particular day, we were given what's called a "Cinderella leave," meaning we had to be back on the ship by midnight. Most of us made it back on board before our carriage reverted to a pumpkin, but a couple of my fellow SEALs did not. One of those men is one of my best buddies, Scott Rawding.

As Scott tells the story, he and a fellow SEAL arrived at around one o'clock in the morning, only to spot our ship—the USS *Hermitage*, a large Navy amphibious landing ship—had moved away from the dock and was anchored half a mile offshore. Not wanting to be court-martialed for going AWOL, Scott and his friend did what any self-respecting Navy SEAL would do in such a predicament: they stripped off their clothes and began swimming out to their ship. Their plan was to climb up the anchor chain, a distance of about 150 feet nearly straight up, and sneak on board before anyone noticed they were missing.

To keep their uniforms dry, a key detail in maintaining the ruse, they did a bionic sidestroke the entire way, swimming with one arm while using the other arm to hold their uniforms and shoes up in the air. The chilling midnight Mediterranean water exposed them to hyperthermia, so every minute was crucial. Things went well until they got about halfway to the ship. That's when they were hit by a dangerous riptide that started pushing them sideways, parallel to the ship. And this time, no Coronado gods were watching, ready to snatch their bodies out of danger.

Scott increased his stroke to compensate and was miraculously swept into the ship's gangplank. The shocked sailors on watch above shone a spotlight on him and demanded he identify himself. Scott pleaded with them not to shoot, explaining that he was posted on the ship and had missed the last boat ride back. He climbed—still buck naked—aboard the quarterdeck, and stood as tall and proud as an overconfident peacock. He saluted the officer on watch and asked permission to board. The officer, attempting to keep a straight face, demanded to know which unit Scott was with (over a hundred men were on the ship). When Scott told him, the officer ordered him to go directly to his quarters. Scott had been anticipating a court-martial or some other sort of on board punishment, so the fact that he was merely ordered to his quarters was a tremendous relief.

Meanwhile, his buddy Billy was having a worse ordeal. A

weaker swimmer, he was exhausted from his fight against the rip-tide. Still, he somehow made it to the ship's anchor chain and started to climb. This was far harder than he had anticipated. He discovered the chain was covered with thick black grease to enable it to slide smoothly while being laid out or taken in. In the chilling night wind, Billy managed to struggle halfway up—about seventy feet. Falling from that height could kill him. Alone high in the air in the frigid temperature with little hope, the combined confidence from the alcohol and being a SEAL finally departed from his body. He called for help. Billy got a break that saved his life. The crew on watch heard his cries and deployed a small boat to rescue him and bring him back on board. Miraculously, Billy wasn't court-martialed either.

When I think about this story, I laugh. Only a Navy SEAL would think that climbing a 150-foot anchor chain with three-foot-long links in the early morning hours is a good idea. But I also see it as a tremendous example of grace. Having broken curfew and then trying to sneak onboard, Scott and Billy were deserving of punishment. They knew it, and they were ready to take whatever their commanding officer threw at them. Instead of punishment though, they received grace, a second chance; and they didn't waste it.

This picture of grace, undeserved favor, is exactly what God offers us. Many of us are afraid to approach God. Heaven seems like a formidable ship anchored far from shore, and we hope perhaps that if we sneak through life, maybe we can find a way to climb aboard without being noticed or punished. But this underlying fear needs to be faced.

As all tadpoles who become Navy SEALs know, fear is a barrier to any successful mission. It limits our ability to think clearly and decisively. God knows this. Therefore, He had Paul tell us, "Don't worry about anything; instead, pray about everything. Tell God what you need, and thank him for all he has done. Then you will experience God's peace, which exceeds anything we can understand" (Philippians 4:6–7, NLT).

Tadpoles are always accountable, and they don't blame others, a tactic we see from almost every politician or media journalist today. Tadpoles understand if there's no accountability in war, people die. In other areas of life, relationships die without accountability. Tadpoles also know there are few things as powerful as a sincere "I'm sorry." Hearts are often instantly healed by the utterance of these two words when spoken sincerely.

Like Scott and Billy, all of us deserve punishment for our mistakes; but rather than sneak around in fear, if we confess our sins to God and truly repent, God will meet us with the same reception Scott and Billy encountered that night.

Buck naked and all.

DARE TO SEEK GRACE

- Always take responsibility for your own actions. Do not blame others for your choices. You are accountable.
- Forgive yourself as you would forgive another in your situation.
- Ask honestly for God's grace, and if you are truly repentant, it will be granted.

20

LOCK IN, LOCK OUT, LOCK ON

Tadpole Faith Knows Suffering Produces Perseverance, Character, and Hope

SPENDING A FEW DAYS ABOARD a nuclear submarine like the USS *Skate* was a Byzantine experience. The only thing better was diving out of a fast-moving sub while it was fully submerged, which is necessary sometimes during combat so as not to be spotted by the enemy.

To do so without getting hurt or killed requires careful procedures called "locking in" and "locking out." To begin, a couple of us in full gear would climb a ladder to the top of the sub, then close and screw down the hatch, effectively locking ourselves into a compartment sealed off from the rest of the sub. Then we would fill the hatch with water and slowly vent pressure in to equalize with the pressure of the water outside. We had to do it slowly and with perfect precision to prevent lung embolism—a blockage of one of the pulmonary arteries in the lungs. Once the equalization procedure was complete, we would lock out by departing from the sub hatch door, doing a free ascent to the water's surface, then swimming away on our mission. Once we finished our mission, we returned to the sub and repeated the process in reverse.

Locking in and locking out were familiar concepts for us, helping us get through the BUD/S daily grind. We constantly locked in a positive attitude while locking out all the noise and distractions. The result was a constant get-going, no-excuses resolve as solid as a brick wall, a focus that was ironclad without regard to self-interest. It was like staring down a poisoned-tip spear with your name on it. To be a tadpole meant constant positive motion, moving forward fearlessly without pause.

What I recall most about BUD/S is that whenever pain knocks on a tadpole's front door, he opens it. Tadpoles don't step back, nor do they blink. They default to "go." Pain is often ignored. This is the life of a tadpole. It has to be this way to survive. Tadpoles must be locked in to become SEALs. No distractions allowed. Always in the fight. Never backing down. One goal. One purpose.

Navy SEAL Marcus Luttrell shared the story of an operation on the Afghanistan/Pakistan border in his book *Lone Survivor*. He wrote about one of his fellow SEALs who was fatally shot during a firefight:

> Danny Dietz would not give up in his final moments on this earth in the middle of a firefight and was saturated in blood, still conscious, still trying to fire his rifle at the enemy. But he was in a facedown position. I told him to take it easy while I turned him over. "Come on, Dan, we're going be all right." He nodded, and I knew he could not speak and would probably never speak again. What I really remember is, he would not let go of his rifle. I raised him by the shoulders and hauled him into an almost sitting position. Then, grasping him under the arms, I started to drag him backward, toward cover. And would you believe it, that little iron man opened fire at the enemy once again, almost lying on his back, blasting away up the hill while I kept dragging him.[10]

I often wonder if my faith in Christ is that locked in. Would I continue to defend the name of Jesus while being dragged on my back and under fire?

God can shape a person's character during difficult experiences, all the while building unnerving and lasting faith. "We also glory in our sufferings, because we know that suffering produces perseverance; perseverance, character; and character, hope" (Romans 5:3–4, NIV). Faithful followers of Christ often are thankful for the horrible circumstances that brought them closer to God. Such sufferings can be considered a gift. Joni Eareckson Tada was a nonbeliever until she was paralyzed from a diving accident. She has testified that she'd rather be in a wheelchair knowing God than on her feet without Him.

When I served at the Atlanta Homeless Shelter, I asked a dozen or so men how they could have such a positive attitude during the most difficult time in their lives. One by one, they all shared how thankful they were for the dire circumstances that finally led them to surrender to God. C. S. Lewis in *The Problem of Pain* wrote, "God whispers to us in our pleasures, speaks in our conscience, but shouts in our pains; it is His megaphone to rouse a deaf world."[11] People who've survived horrific circumstances and continue to trust God experience abounding faith.

God may allow some horrible things in our lives because it will help others grow in their faith. Tadpole faith is okay with that. It keeps moving forward. Maybe not at record-breaking speed, but at God's speed. And that's all that matters.

At some point every tadpole surrenders himself. His pain, fear, storms, regrets, and the painful choices made by others are no longer relevant; and he goes for broke for a single purpose. Fear has no hold on his heart. He knows his success depends on locking in all that's required for achieving his purpose—God's purpose—as well as locking out all that isn't. It's the only way I know to lock on to a life that's truly worth living.

DARE TO LOCK IN YOUR FAITH

- Suffering produces perseverance, character, hope and often reveals our purpose.

- A person's character is shaped during life's most turbulent storms.

- Never back down, because it is through life's challenges that your mind and body develop. Scar tissue is better armor than skin.

- In tough times, do I fall into the revolving carousel of self-pity and worry, or into the uncharted waters of God? The first is easy; the latter requires courage.

21

TO SURVIVE, TRAIN HARDER
AND LONGER THAN THE ENEMY

Tadpole Faith Is High-Energy Momentum

FORT A. P. HILL, NEAR Bowling Green, Virginia, is a place where SEALs based on the East Coast go to shoot guns and blow things up. In other words, it's where soldiers go to play. On one occasion while I was training there, Senior Chief Janeka, the platoon chief in our Caribbean detachment, offered a demonstration that rocks my boat even today.

It was late at night, after a full day of shooting, and Senior Chief Janeka came out to the campfire holding a stick of C-4 explosive. All I could think was, *What's he doing walking around an open flame with an explosive powerful enough to knock down a small mountain?* He called out to us, as if he needed to do anything more to get our attention, and held the C-4 in one hand and a lighter in the other. Before our astonished eyes, he lit the C-4, and it began to burn in a wild and beautiful spray of glowing fire. I've never seen the northern lights, but it had to rank up there with them. I couldn't believe my eyes.

I waited for the inevitable explosion and my last glimpse of Senior Chief Janeka before his body was blown to unrecognizable bits of charred bone and tissue, but it never happened. The C-4 just continued to spray glowing fire brighter than you can imagine.

What I should have remembered from my classroom training—but forgot in my panic—is that to make an explosion requires three elements: the C-4, heat (such as fire), and a concussion, such as that provided by a blasting cap. Even if Senior Chief Janeka had dropped the fiery C-4, it probably wouldn't have been enough of an impact to cause it to explode—not that I would have dared try it. That's why you'll always find a detonation cord attached to a shiny metallic object, a blasting cap, buried inside a stick of dynamite or plastic explosive.

In the same way, having an explosive faith—one that can move mountains—requires three key elements. The first is God's Word. This is equivalent to C-4. It has the potential to detonate an explosion that can be felt by everyone who knows you. But for that power to be unleashed, the Bible can't just sit there on the shelf. You have to read it and meditate on it, so the words leap off the page and into your soul.

The second element is prayer. Prayer is equivalent to the heat required to ignite the C-4. Prayer opens up the pathway between you and God, kindling the flame of the Holy Spirit in your heart.

The final element is action. This is the blasting cap. As James 2:26 tells us, "Faith without deeds is dead" (NIV). If all we do is read the Bible and pray, we'll be no more effective than Senior Chief Janeka standing there by the campfire clutching the burning C-4. We might look pretty, with colorful flames billowing in the night; but when it comes to exploding the enemy's strongholds, we'll be utterly ineffective.

Tadpoles are not lazy; it's not in their DNA. Their momentum constantly pushes them from one action to the next. They're hustlers, go-getters. They know they were created to excel. Their minds work nonstop on what is good, pure, and purposeful; and they're always moving forward. Likewise, Christ followers continuously drive forward with the same energy as though their lives are a witness to many.

God's Word, prayer, and action—there's no more explosive combination than that.

DARE TO ACT OUT YOUR FAITH

- Never be content with mediocrity. Most people are ordinary and hate it.
- The extra mile alone is not enough. Real leaders are ordinary people with extraordinary determination. Go the extra thousand.
- Define yourself by your own "wow factor," and the results will come. Want more? Strive for God's "wow!"

22

A CULTURE OF GRATITUDE

Tadpole Faith Is Crazy Grateful

ONE OF THE DREAM JOBS I had following BUD/S—aside from representing the Navy at a Miss America pageant—was helping set the diving tables for the Draeger LAR-V closed-loop diving system. Also known as a rebreather, the Draeger is an underwater breathing apparatus that absorbs the carbon dioxide from a diver's breath to permit rebreathing, which is recycling the substantial amount of unused oxygen in each exhaled breath. The advantage of the system, especially when it comes to combat diving, is that it eliminates the telltale bubbles that can give away a diver's location during a clandestine operation.

The job required three guys from the East Coast teams and three guys from the West Coast teams to stay on the campus of Duke University for six months, during which we underwent tests in the basement of the Duke University hospital two or three days each week. The tests took place in a six-by-ten-foot water tank with nothing but a couple of tiny portholes offering us a view of the outside. It could be an anxiety-ridden, claustrophobic experience. In essence, we were human guinea pigs, our bodies covered with patches and stuck full of needles to monitor the oxygen levels in our blood during each four- to five-hour dive.

Because we had to work only two or three days a week, we had plenty of time to do other things. I took on two part-time jobs during my time there: bartending and dance instructing. I was paid to serve up tropical drinks with cute little umbrellas in them and to teach people how to swing dance. And not just any people—pretty girls.

Before teaching, I had rhythm, but I hadn't had any formal instruction. The dance school took care of that in a hurry, and soon I was one of their top instructors. When one of the dance students was asked about her goals, she replied, "To learn to dance like Larry." After a compliment like that, combined with the strong sense of self-confidence I already felt from graduating BUD/S, it's amazing that my head could fit inside that gigantic diving tank.

As fun as being a popular dance instructor was, it was also a good reminder of how easy it is to get carried away with pride. Making decisions that build confidence and a sense of satisfaction in your achievements is one thing, but when you go beyond that and think your achievements actually make you better than others, you're in dangerous territory. Pride precedes a fall.

Such ungratefulness reminds me of the well-dressed man sipping drinks in a bar one night. When the polite waitress asked him why he was so sad, he replied, "My uncle died two months ago and left me $500,000 in oil wells. Then another uncle died last month and left me $100,000 in stocks."

"I'm sorry, you must have been very close to your uncles."

"No, not at all. I barely knew them."

"Then why are you so unhappy?" the waitress asked, confused.

"So far this month, no one has died and left me a cent."

Winston Churchill was once asked if he was thrilled that every time he gave a speech, the hall was packed to overflowing. "It's quite flattering," he replied, "but I always remember that if instead of making a political speech I was being hanged, the crowd would be twice as big."

Living a life full of gratefulness is not easy, but the easy life is never worth following. One of the purest measures of a person's life is his or her ability to inspire others. That requires a heart of unshakeable gratitude. It also means loving others no matter the odds, even if doing so brings pain, like Jesus' raging wounds in His wrists and feet.

I'm proud to have played a small role in the development of the Draeger system—I'm also happy to have had the opportunity to dance with all those girls at Duke. But I'm humbled every time I think that no matter what skill or ability I have, I can't claim responsibility for any of them, and I thank God for blessing me with the gifts I've been given.

DARE TO BE GRATEFUL

- Gratefulness is a decision, not a lucky feeling.
- Be grateful for what you have because you have resources, and be grateful for what you don't have because it lights your fire.
- Be ready to use the gifts God has given you to take a stand for others when there is injustice.

23

RECOVERING BOLDNESS— JUST IN TIME

Tadpole Faith Is Blissfully Spontaneous

My personal confidence after graduating BUD/S was at an all-time high. The only opinion that mattered was my own. That wasn't a good place to be, but God has a way of redeeming us at our worst moments.

Following the four years in the Navy, I needed some time away, so I decided to spend a weekend with a friend in Minneapolis. At the end of our visit, I caught a connecting flight to Cincinnati, planning to continue back home from there to Washington, DC.

I arrived at the airport gate in Cincinnati, unclean and unshaven, cheap pink shower shoes—flip-flops. I didn't care what other people thought of me. All I knew was that I had a first-class ticket and free drinks all the way home.

As boarding commenced, I approached the Delta departure gate and noticed a gorgeous flight attendant. Her stunning beauty and drop-dead gorgeous smile caused my heart to miss a few beats. I began to wish I'd combed my hair that morning. I wasn't even certain I'd brushed my teeth. For the first time since graduating from BUD/S and going into the teams, I felt anxious—human. I knew she was out of my league; however, like any smart, dashing single guy, I tried to think up some clever words that would knock her off her feet (rather than cause me to foolishly trip over my own). Getting her attention would not be an easy task since I assumed she'd heard all the fast lines while dashing from city to city. I had to remind myself that I was likely not the only guy who had been dazzled by her. And I was wearing pink shower shoes, for goodness' sake!

I immediately went to work on my confidence. I reminded myself that I was a certifiable Navy Special Forces operator, and I wasn't half bad-looking. I had a first-class ticket, meaning she would have to be extra kind to me. Maybe she would be impressed. How could she not notice the confidence I carried? At least that's what I told myself.

As I took my seat, I noted she was serving the first-class cabin. By God's grace, she couldn't ignore me now. And, as luck would have it, only one other passenger was in the first-class cabin. I could hear the angels urging me on. All I needed was to make a good, memorable first impression.

Knowing Delta's headquarters was in Atlanta, after two hours of working up the courage to speak to this beautiful woman, my brilliant mind came up with only one question: "Are you Atlanta-based?"

As soon as those words escaped my lips, I realized how lame they were. But it was too late to grab them back. I must have already turned three shades of red.

Her answer was as cordial as it was thorough: "Yes."

She walked back to the galley, leaving me sitting there mentally beating myself up. Any conversationalist worth his salt knows never to ask a yes-or-no closed-end question.

Minutes after, the pilot made a horrid announcement: "We're now approaching Washington, DC. Passengers, please buckle up, and flight attendants collect all service items."

I couldn't believe I'd blown my one and only chance. I'd let fear and its ugly cousin, anxiety, dominate. It was as if everything my SEAL training had instilled in me had evaporated.

While all the other passengers were buckling their seat belts, I saw that she was cleaning up the first-class galley on her own. With the plane quickly descending and only minutes until we landed, I was desperate to make a positive impression. Still seated, I shyly glanced back to see if any other flight attendants were approaching. They were not. I'd been given another chance to make a good impression without making a fool of myself in front of others. One last hope. It was a now-or-never moment.

Dale Carnegie once said, "Inaction breeds doubt and fear. Action breeds confidence and courage. If you want to conquer fear, do not sit home and think about it. Go out and get busy."[12] Without a second thought, I unbuckled my seat belt and stormed the galley, saying the first words that came to my mind: "Either you're going to move to Washington, or I'm moving to Atlanta. Which is it going to be?"

Her enchanting smile was a fulfilled dream. No more words were needed.

She said she'd never given her number to a passenger before, but out came her pen. In the normal world, I would have thought, *Yeah, sure, as if she'd actually give me her real number.* But I sensed she was different. I believed her.

I called her at once. It was about 2:00 a.m. when she arrived at her home following her Washington-to-Atlanta flight. We talked for a couple of hours, till almost daybreak, and then with even more intensity over the next few days. The following weekend she visited me in Washington, and from there we flew directly to Chattanooga to meet my family.

Twenty-five years later, here we are, still happily dating and married. No doubt it wasn't the pickup line that got me to the dance; it was refusing to give in to my social fears and finally finding the confidence to walk up and talk to her. Ironically, I learned later that not only had Deb done everything in her power not to be on that particular flight (she'd been trying to rearrange her schedule so she could attend a Kenny G concert), she'd also tried to get out of serving the first-class cabin (which, thankfully, had nothing to do with me).

Every decision leads to a destination. Some decisions require us to be bold. Others require sacrifice. None should require us to wear pink flip-flops.

As Christians, we have to be alert and get busy! We have to remain vigilant for God's purpose. This means making eye contact, conversing with sincere interest, and giving of yourself even if it's uncomfortable. Tadpoles constantly reach out to others without first being reached. They smile with the purpose of planting seeds of joy, peace, and happiness in the hearts of all others. They understand that the power of one person who genuinely desires to lift up others has the utmost potential to make a gigantic difference, no matter how small or large the reward may be. These same attributes are honored even in the secular world, where eighty-five percent of job promotions are due more to these positive attitudes than to skill.[13]

I don't like to think of where I'd be today if I hadn't unbuckled my seat belt and boldly approached that lovely flight attendant who became my bride. Greater than that is the decision I make every day to serve God's glorious name. No matter where He calls me, I'll unbuckle my seat belt and follow with blind boldness. It's called trusting Him. Psalm 16:8 is a great reminder during such bold moments when we tend to blink, as I did that one unforgettable day: "I know the LORD is always with me. I will not be shaken, for he is right beside me" (NLT).

A life imitating Christ isn't easy. But then, the easy life is not worth living.

DARE TO BE BOLD

- You can and should have the confidence to own any room you enter, regardless of how you felt before you opened that door—not because of who you are but whose you are.

- You have the capability to create a new culture and inspire. By the same token, you are also allowed to move on when it is time.

- Make others feel special, because at the end of the day, it's relationships that matter.

24

EVEN YOUNG LIONS GO HUNGRY

Tadpole Faith Screams What Is True, Honorable,
Right, and Pure

WHEN I WAS NINETEEN YEARS old, my summer job was selling accident insurance from door to door. It was a cheap, no-frills policy for people who normally had no accident insurance. Needless to say, long hot days filled with rejections did not make for an enjoyable summer. Nevertheless, it taught me the value of keeping a positive mental attitude in the face of adversity.

In our training for the job, the other salesmen and I were instructed to carry out a ritual before leaving to pound the pavement each morning. We were to look into the mirror and shout, "I feel healthy, I feel happy, I feel terrific!" a minimum of twenty-five times. Then we went out and followed it up with "affirmative action"—which, back then, meant knocking on doors.

The average person has about 70,000 thoughts each day. Just think of the powerful, constant influence our thoughts have over our lives. Every action and every belief begins with a single thought, an idea. So does every achievement—and every failure. So did it work to yell a positive mantra to myself each morning? Absolutely. I always walked out of my home smiling, and because

I started out with a positive attitude, it took a long time for the constant stream of rejection to beat me down.

Clearly, God had our best interest in mind when He inspired the apostle Paul to write the following words: "Finally, brothers and sisters, whatever is true, whatever is noble, whatever is right, whatever is pure, whatever is lovely, whatever is admirable—if anything is excellent or praiseworthy—*think about such things*" (Philippians 4:8, NIV).

It's not always easy to maintain constant positive thoughts. It's as if a hacker is camping out deep inside your brain, just waiting for the opportunity to install a toxic virus that threatens to eventually take down the entire mainframe. Such invasive, lingering thoughts can lead to a lack of sleep, self-doubt, guilt, and anxiety. Worse, they can rob you of joy and take you off your game of loving like Jesus and sharing His love with others.

If you want to defeat such thoughts, you must accept the fact that this is a choice. There were a billion reasons not to succeed in BUD/S, but I succeeded by focusing on the prize and keeping my thoughts on a winning track. I had to remind myself that God created each of us to run for the prize. The same was true in business, whether I was selling insurance policies or the software I developed once my duty to the Navy was over.

Since the human mind cannot think two thoughts at the same time, all you need to do once a "hacker" inserts a toxic code into your mind is to instantly transfer to a preset positive thought. The key is to not allow Satan and his hit squad to infect your mind, and the best way to do that is to fill your mind with thoughts of God. To do this, I use what I call the "two-second pivot rule." This means that whenever a bad thought enters my mind, I immediately pivot away to a positive thought. It's like being on automatic during Hell Week, or what politicians do whenever they're asked tough questions they don't want to answer. I don't give the negative thought any real estate in my mind beyond two seconds. This works well because the human brain can focus on only one thought at a time.

The next time Satan attempts to hack your thoughts, emulate what I did every morning while selling insurance and proclaim God's promises: "I'm God's treasure, I'm God's masterpiece, and I'm created to win!" In fact, it's worth repeating those words many times throughout the day, not just in the morning!

Better yet, if you know God's Word, do what Jesus did when Satan tempted Him. He replied, "It is written . . ." and quoted Scripture. "The devil took him to a very high mountain and showed him all the kingdoms of the world and their splendor. 'All this I will give you,' he said, 'if you will bow down and worship me.' Jesus said to him, 'Away from me, Satan! For it is written: "Worship the Lord your God, and serve him only."'" Then the devil left him, and angels came and attended him" (Matthew 4:8–11, NIV).

Your mind is a battlefield. But how you think and what you think is up to you because you're the one who decides what to allow into your mind. God gave you control over your thoughts. You're in charge. You rule. Do you have problems with impure thoughts? Then figure out how they're getting into your mind, whether it's through movies, television, games, conversation, friends, or whatever.

Every battle you fight is won or lost in your head before you take any action. Therefore, don't concede the fight before it's even begun. "Be sober-minded; be watchful. Your adversary the devil prowls around like a roaring lion, seeking someone to devour" (1 Peter 5:8, ESV). Protect your mind, and fill it with whatever is true, honorable, right, pure, lovely, admirable, and worthy of praise, and there'll be no room left for Satan to snake his way in.

About ninety percent of people's behavior is habitual, meaning our lives are most often dictated by routine. John Maxwell said, "Most people stop themselves from reaching their potential."[14] Take a mental inventory of your daily habits. What you read or watch, the friends you keep, and your routine thoughts are who you are and become.

Whenever a tadpole rang out, it was rarely one evolution that led him to that decision. It was the ongoing negative thoughts and doubts that encroached long before he rang the bell. Somewhere along the line, he made a decision that let them in.

In life, ringing out is giving in to sin. Ask God to replace negative thoughts—every day and every moment—with whatever is true, honorable, right, and pure. It takes practice, so don't give up, and don't ring out! Being one in Christ is always worth the fight.

DARE TO THINK POSITIVELY

- What you allow into your mind dictates what comes out in the form of actions. How you think is everything.

- Protect your thought life. Make it a daily habit to repeat encouraging words of empowerment to maintain a positive attitude.

- Fill your mind with God's Word, and there will be no room left for Satan to fill it with his lies, doubts, and fears.

25

WHEN YOU'RE DOWN TO NOTHING, GOD IS UP TO SOMETHING

Tadpole Faith Never Lets Suffering Go to Waste

I WAS NEVER A GREAT student, but I wasn't exactly the slowest car in the heat either, so when I was pulled from my elementary school class of about thirty students one day to join a smaller group of five or so other students, my radar started to ping. Even at ten years of age, I saw bogies on the horizon! No one explained anything to me, and even if they had, I probably wouldn't have understood. Now, dozens of programs recognize and treat the variety of opportunities (I don't believe in problems—only opportunities) struggling students have in school, but back then it was more of a one-size-fits-all approach.

If I was in school today, I probably would be diagnosed with some form of attention-deficit disorder. My attention span lasts no more than a flash before I'm fast-forwarding to my next project. That attribute was an advantage in my business because it kept me looking forward instead of dwelling on past mistakes and failures. It also helped me get through BUD/S. Unfortunately, such "opportunities" aren't regarded as foundational to academic success.

As I continued through school, I noticed I was often in different classes than my friends were in, but I never asked why. Then one summer afternoon on the last day of seventh grade, I opened my final report card, and on the back it read "Retained." I took a second glance, hoping that "Retained" meant something other than the dark, achy feeling that began to form in the bottom of my stomach.

By the time I arrived home, I'd never felt so much like a failure. According to that piece of paper, I literally *was* a failure. My parents weren't home, but one of my good buddies came over to celebrate the fact that school was out, so I shared the news with him. His response continues to echo in my heart whenever I'm feeling low: "You're dumb, but you're not *that* dumb." My small world was shattered. I'd be held back to repeat the seventh grade as my friends moved on. The embarrassment, shame, and loneliness I felt were enormous.

Things changed the following year when I got the help I needed to perform well in school. But the enemy loves to prey on easy targets, like a shark scenting blood. I recall my English teacher bragging about my newfound achievements in her class one day. A fellow student looked straight at me and said, "Yeah, but this is your second year doing this work." I couldn't muster a reply. She was smart, pretty, and popular. And she was right.

Just as God uses people to do His work, so does the enemy. Neither my good buddy nor the girl in that class would remember their comments if I asked them today, but their words have stuck with me. Fifty years later, they're still ready to pounce whenever my self-confidence is called into question.

I'm beyond thankful that God continued to love me and never left my side after I received that daunting report card. I know now that God uses all of our disappointments, shame, and failures for His glory. As the Coronado gods taught us, adversity introduces a man to himself. But failure doesn't introduce us only to ourselves; it also introduces us to God. Through failure, we realize our weaknesses, our limitations, and our need to rely absolutely on our creator.

We shouldn't be afraid of mistakes. As actress Tallulah Bankhead once said, "If I had my life to live again, I would make the same mistakes, only sooner."

No doubt, all of us have experienced people saying hurtful words that stung, words that can hurt for years, even decades. Worse is when we think and tell those hurtful things to ourselves. This I do know: anything intended to hurt or pull me down is not from God but from the enemy.

All tadpoles know that to become a SEAL they have to be mentally strong and constantly running at 1,000 percent. Since I love Jesus, I know He has big plans for me. I'm so grateful that through God I've found an out. It's called forgiveness—when you put on your Jesus backpack and move forward. I'm determined to make a difference, and there's no room in my backpack for trash. Today, hurtful comments only propel me to remain fighter-pilot-focused, believing only what God says about me because I know the source of those comments.

When Christ was hanging on the cross, He appeared to be at His weakest point, abandoned by His friends and completely at the mercy of His enemies. His disciples were also at their lowest moment. Three days later, God showed His divine power, and humankind was changed forever. God is always willing and waiting to show His divine power, even when it looks as if He's powerless or invisible. We can cling to the cross. We can focus on *Him*.

This life is only a snap of the finger. Like any tadpole during Hell Week, no matter how dazed, desperate, or confused we are or how devastated by life's tragedies, we can rest assured, knowing disappointment and pain are temporal, and God will be at our side forever, cheering us on.

With God at my side, I started working more diligently on

my academics. Not only did my grades reflect my hard work but later on, when I sold insurance for a summer job and took the insurance exam, I scored the highest test score in the state. I owe a good part of that success to my friend for that kick in the heart of calling me dumb. But I'm most thankful to God for picking me up and not allowing me to feel sorry for myself. My life has been unimaginably blessed. God has never left me alone.

In seasons when tadpoles face failure, broken relationships, loss, and grief, they tend to vigorously find meaning and purpose that will ultimately exceed such painful trials. They never let any suffering go to waste.

Life is filled with reasons to throw a pity party. After all, self-pity is the safest and easiest response to adversity. Failure and rejection can act as a trapdoor, imprisoning us deep down in the darkness, where all we do is feel sorry for ourselves. Instead, God commands us to walk not in the flesh but in the Spirit, which means abiding in Him. As Christ followers, we can face every trial with the boldness of Jesus, knowing He's always faithful.

DARE TO FIND MOTIVATION IN SUFFERING

- Don't define your life according to the trials and struggles you are experiencing.
- What others may tell you is a weakness or shortcoming can often prove to be a strength in other parts of your life.
- Remember that adversity is like a refining fire, preparing you for greater victories in the days ahead.

26

THE JOY IN BEING HOMELESS

Tadpole Faith Finds Common Ground with Everyone

ONE OF THE QUALITIES I admire most about my bride, that gorgeous airline attendant who actually married me, is that she's just as comfortable serving the poor as she is serving the rich and famous. Some call this humility. I call it being like Jesus. Thankfully, some of Deb's graciousness and humility has rubbed off on me.

Early in our marriage, Deb and I lived in Dallas, but once we started having children, we moved to Atlanta to be closer to family. However, I had such a great staff that I decided to keep the office in Dallas, even though this meant I had to travel there every few months. Rather than being a liability, the arrangement gave me the opportunity to experience God's richness by calling me out of my comfort zone.

While in Dallas, I would drive downtown after work and park my car a few blocks from the Dallas Life Foundation, a shelter for men. I always went alone, known to no one but God. I wanted to be entirely dependent on God. Any courage or fear I felt was His to bear. He was my sole swim buddy. I would put on some Goodwill-style duds and then check myself in as a homeless man. After being on several mission trips, I knew I could never find true common ground unless they saw me as their equal. And I believe it's safe to say so did the God of the universe in the life of Jesus Christ. My goal was to meet, pray with, and encourage as many men as God led me to meet. I didn't want to take up one of the shelter's valuable beds, so I'd quietly depart prior to lights out.

I would often walk up to homeless men and engage them in conversation. Ideally, I would listen while also seeking opportunities to offer seeds of encouragement and the good news of Jesus. Then, as the conversation was ending, I would casually mention that I would love to treat the man to lunch sometime. You can imagine the startled look on each man's face since I was supposedly just as broke as they were. I would shake their hands—with a twenty-dollar bill buried in my palm. Their reaction to the small gift was priceless. I did that for a couple of years, and I always walked away feeling blessed.

One night at the Dallas Life Foundation—upstairs, where the hundred or so beds are located—I asked God to lead me to anyone with whom He wanted me to engage. It was late, and I noticed a tall, skinny man seemingly in his sixties lying on his twin-size bed wearing nothing but boxer shorts and cowboy boots. He was reading a small New Testament. I thanked God for being so prompt and journeyed through the sea of beds to introduce myself.

The man told me his name was Bob. We chatted and engaged like the brothers we were. The other men around us must have thought we were close kin because of the way we were hooting and laughing it up.

When we finished our visit, I asked Bob if I could pray for any of his needs. He turned his head and scanned the large room filled with a hundred or so homeless men. Then he looked me straight in the eye. "All of my needs are already met," he said.

Bob likely didn't have a dime to his name. All his belongings were hanging from the side of his bed in a plastic grocery bag. But at that moment, he was more content than I was with all my abundant earthly possessions. In moments like these, how can we not embrace God's reminder in Galatians 6:3, "If you think you are too important to help someone, you are only fooling yourself. You are not that important" (NLT).

My eyes were filled with tears as I walked away. Isn't it just like God to do that? As we go to serve others, He turns it around and blesses us instead. I'm so thankful for the moments when God reminds me of what's truly important in life. I love finding common ground with everyone. The best part is, whenever I do it, God always finds common ground with me.

DARE TO FIND COMMON GROUND WITH EVERYONE

- Look for what you share in common with others, not what makes you different from one another.
- Go places where you may be needed and seek out ways you can help.
- Remain open to the gifts God wants to bring you, especially when helping others.

27

THE GREATEST COMMANDMENT

*Tadpole Faith Means Knowing that Joy Means
Living Beyond Self*

THROUGHOUT MY LIFE, I'VE SEEN times of plenty and times of want. I know firsthand what it's like to be hungry, so during times of financial prosperity, Deb and I tend to share our windfall with those who are in need. I should add that we also relish a good surprise, especially when Jesus can get all the credit.

Perhaps my favorite period of life was when God blessed us financially to the point that Deb and I were able to purchase automobiles for people who needed them. I would ask the car dealer to drive the new car to the recipient's home, park it in their driveway, and then knock on their front door. When they answered, he was to hand them the keys. Then I would add, "Oh yeah, one more thing, you cannot reveal who purchased the car for them. Naturally, God gets all the credit here."

When you come across an opportunity to help someone, do it in secret. As Jesus says, "When you give to the needy, do not announce it with trumpets, as the hypocrites do in the synagogues and on the streets, to be honored by others. Truly I tell you, they have received their reward in full. But when you give to the needy, do not let your left hand know what your right hand is doing, so that your giving may be in secret. Then your Father, who sees what is done in secret, will reward you" (Matthew 6:2–4, NIV).

I never saw the moment when someone received their car. But I once accidentally came close. I was attending an event with a missionary friend on the day before a new car we'd purchased was to be delivered to him. The car dealer happened to be a contributor to my friend, and during our ride home together, my friend saw he had left a voicemail saying he needed to meet with him about an important matter the following day. I looked on innocently as my friend listened to the voicemail and then looked feverishly ahead as he was driving. He shook his head, a grim look on his face.

"This can't be good news," he said.

I remained stoic, but I was bursting inside. If I played poker for a living, I would have cleaned up that day. It was all I could do to keep my secret. It made me think about how God's grace is so amazing!

You may not have the means to bless someone with a new vehicle, but you have a lot you can offer. Look for the needs you can fill for others. Maybe you have the means to pay for someone's meal—ask the server for their check and pay it along with yours (tip included) just before you leave. Place a little treat on the desk of a busy, stressed coworker to brighten their day. Offer to give a ride or pick up groceries for a friend or neighbor that has trouble getting to the supermarket. Search online for local volunteer opportunities, and sign up to help out. Remember that often it's the fact that someone noticed their need and did something for them that matters to others more than what you gave.

A retiring missionary was coming home to America on the same boat as the president of the United States. Cheering crowds, a military band, a red carpet, banners, and the media welcomed the president home, but the missionary slipped off the ship unnoticed. Feeling self-pity and resentment, he began complaining to God. Then God gently reminded him, "But, My child, you're not home yet." Tadpole faith is all about radical focus on others rather than self. It's all about making life count. This kind of love doesn't waver. It never dies.

One last thought about giving to others, and it won't cost you a penny. It's also perhaps the best way to reflect God's light all the time. Next time you come across a service worker, such as a waiter or barista, who seems to be neglecting you or is vaguely rude, offer them a smile rather than a glare. Ask them if you can be of any help to them. Yes, it may be a little bold, but I've never had a waiter become upset when I turn the tables and seek to serve them. It's possible they are having a horrible day or going through a difficult time in their life and need some kindness. Anyone can love people who are good to them, but it takes being like Jesus to love those who need it most, especially at their worst moments. You'll be amazed at how God can show up in a nanosecond. This is a demonstration of God's call to love others as we love ourselves.

Tadpole faith becomes tadpole love.

DARE TO BLESS OTHERS

- Remain vigilant for small—and big—ways you can help others.
- Share the blessings you have, whether that's money, a skill, or just a listening ear.
- The act of giving will transform you in the process, making you more loving than you were before.

28

A NEW DEFINITION OF "NFL"

Tadpole Faith Is Wired for Success

A DEAR YOUNG FRIEND AND one-time neighbor of mine, David Andrews, is the starting center for the New England Patriots of the National Football League. I remember David as a high schooler playing with my youngest son, Avery, who was in middle school. When he was recruited by the University of Georgia, I was honored to have him show up at my door to share the great news. I remember mentioning to David's coach at Georgia, Mark Richt, how interesting it was that David could be a starting lineman with a top-ranked Southeastern Conference football team and still be such a nice kid. Coach Richt responded that David is one of those kids who can turn the aggression on and off like a light switch. He's an animal on the field and a gentleman as soon as he gets off it.

Once David fulfilled his dream of playing for the Super Bowl champs, the New England Patriots, I assumed he felt secure, that he was finally living the good life. But recently David told me what else the acronym NFL stands for: "Not For Long." He wakes up every day recognizing there's a chance he could be cut from the team or, worse, sustain an injury that takes him out for a game or a season, or even brings his career to a permanent halt. The average career for a pro football lineman can be as short as

135

four years. Imagine being a well-known success in the eyes of the world one moment, earning a top one percent income, and then in a flash you're without a future. It happens to all sorts of professional athletes every year, especially football players. The sad part is, once they get on the gravy train, many of them assume it's going to last forever, so when their ride comes to an abrupt halt, they're totally unprepared.

According to *Sports Illustrated,* seventy-eight percent of National Football League players are either bankrupt or under financial stress within two years of retirement, and an estimated sixty percent of National Basketball Association players go bankrupt within five years after leaving their sport. The same thing could happen to any of us, but the great news is that God provides us with the ultimate insurance to sleep soundly no matter how precarious our circumstances might be. All faithful tadpoles know that sudden disasters are only skin deep. None are permanent.

"Not For Long" applies to us all. Even those of us who live to be a hundred are but a wisp of smoke in the wind, here for a moment and then gone for eternity. Rather than get comfortable and assume the status quo will continue without fail, we should live each day to its fullest, making the most of every opportunity and giving our best effort for the team while we still can.

As in sports, life has seasons. Each season is part of the journey on which God has set us. Enjoy these seasons, learn from them, grow from them, and be excited at the beginning of each new adventure. Be a forward thinker. Remember, goals are important, but they're not nearly as important as your God-given purpose. Purpose trumps all goals.

Build up your identity in Christ and acknowledge that you're an heir to God's kingdom. So many of us get stuck in allowing the world to shape who we think we are. We peg our identity to a title at work, a last name, the number of likes on our latest social media post, our partner, or the size of our bank account. Your true identity is your faith, your values, and your beliefs.

I've had my share of worldly success. But this I can promise: Bank accounts will fluctuate. Jobs and their titles will be earned and lost. Property can be given to someone else, and in time it surely will be. Your body will not always be the same. And in all likelihood, your accomplishments will one day be forgotten. Highlight reels have a tendency to flicker and fade; they don't last forever.

In college, James Dobson's goal was to become the school's tennis champion. He felt proud when his trophy was prominently placed in the school's trophy cabinet. Years later, someone mailed him that trophy. They'd found it in a trash can when the school was remodeled. Jim said, "Given enough time, all your trophies will be trashed by someone else."

But there's great news that I'm bursting to boast about: your real Dad, the one who first created you, has a title for you that will never be tarnished or forgotten. You were predestined by God to obtain an inheritance, called to be an heir with Christ, a saint, and His treasure. You're His chosen and blameless child, forgiven of all your sins no matter what the enemy whispers into your ears. Your title of Child of God will never be given away, and your spirit will never die.

You never know what God has in store for you or how long you have left on this planet. So whatever you feel God calling you to do, get going!

You're wired by the creator of heaven and earth for success— *His* success. Forever!

DARE TO EMBRACE TODAY

- Our identity shouldn't come from our title, bank account or even the mirror; such things will fade away. Your identity must be in Christ.

- See life through the windshield, not the rearview mirror.

- We're not here for a good time or a long time. We're here for precisely the amount of time God has given us to do the tasks He has laid out for us. So don't waste time.

- Treat every day like the gift it is, and make the most of your time by investing in others.

29

DON'T MESS WITH
MOTHERS-IN-LAW

Tadpole Faith Laughs Big

I HAD THE PRIVILEGE OF working with motivational author and speaker Zig Ziglar, who was one of my first marketing consultation clients. When it came to being a Christian, he was the real deal. He was also the first person who showed me that Christianity wasn't about being long-faced and boring. Christians could be financially successful, full of life, and fun.

Life gets pretty serious for Christians who are weighed down with worry. We forget that God created humor for a reason. Considering all the struggles and challenges we face in life, sometimes laughter is the only sane response.

Paul Evancoe was one of my favorite SEAL platoon commanders. He's well known in the SEAL community as a superior operator. I remember him best for his zest for life, a zeal that knew few boundaries when it came to gags. He played one memorable practical joke on his friend and fellow officer, Mr. Blakston.** Like the rat sandwich, such pranks are sometimes necessary to balance the worst circumstances in wartime situations.

** Name changed to protect his identity.

Mr. Blakston was one of my favorite assistant platoon leaders. The man gave the appearance of being highly academic. He loved to smoke his favorite curved pipe. He was slow to speak, and when he did speak, he gave the impression of being a stoic history professor. Because of his sweet-tempered personality, he was a surefire target for practical jokes.

Paul Evancoe knew that Mr. Blakston was going to be flying back to Virginia Beach from Rosy Roads, Puerto Rico, and that he always smoked his pipe on the flight. (Thirty years ago, smoking on a plane was okay.) Sure enough, during the trip Mr. Blakston politely asked the lady next to him if it would be okay for him to light up, and she said it was fine.

A distinguished-looking, professorial man, he pulled out his briefcase with the exacting precision of an assassin and placed it neatly on his lap. After confidently filling his pipe with tobacco, he lit up. To his and everyone else's amazement, rather than the sweet smell of pipe tobacco, a foul odor swamped the first-class cabin. The smell was so noxious that the lady next to him quietly got up and found another seat. To make matters worse, the woman was the Navy base captain's wife from Mr. Blakston's duty station in Rosy Roads!

What Mr. Blakston had failed to notice was that before the flight, his good SEAL buddy, Paul Evancoe, had exchanged his pipe tobacco with a byproduct that comes from the back end of an animal.

Not nearly as exciting, but nevertheless funny, is a practical joke I pulled on my in-laws that eventually turned us into local celebrities. It all started when I decided to have a portrait painted of our four boys all wearing the same outfit. It was similar to other pictures you see of children from that era, with the boys all wearing blue jeans, black shirts, and no shoes.

Finding it humorous to mimic us, my in-laws had their portrait taken, all of them wearing the same clothing. My wife's mother, her sister and brother, their spouses, children, and even her grandmother agreed to the caper. But the exclamation point was that in the photo they were all grimacing. The dig did not end there. They used the photo for their Christmas cards.

In response, I went even bigger—literally. I took the photo off their Christmas card and used it to create a billboard—fourteen feet high and forty-eight feet wide, occupying 672 square feet—overlooking the busiest main street in their city.

Can you imagine their shock driving through town and seeing that billboard?

Someone called the newspaper, and a reporter interviewed them about our pranks. The capers finally came to an abrupt end when my mother-in-law cut and pasted my headshot on an almost naked image on the following year's Christmas card and sent it to all my friends. I surrendered.

I can't tell you how much fun our families had with all this. Such jokes create lasting memories that rarely fade.

Of course, gags can go a little too far. Some American soldiers rented a house during the Korean War and hired a local boy to do their cooking and cleaning. This boy was full of life and had a jovial face, even when the American soldiers teased him almost daily with a new trick. One day they nailed his shoes to the floor. Another day they placed grease on the oven doors. They even placed buckets of water over his door so that when he came in, he got drenched.

Finally, the day arrived when the Americans apologized to the young boy and told him they would never trick him again. The polite young boy replied, "Okay then, I'll no longer spit in your soup."

Laughter isn't just fun; it's also healthy. God created us so that laughing releases endorphins that create a vigorous, energetic, and healthier body. I believe any person can become 100 percent better-looking in an instant, anytime they choose, without spending a dime on cosmetic surgery. How? By smiling more often. A sincere smile can capture and change hearts and minds.

Our creator made laughter for a purpose. Choose friends who are serious about the things that matter, but make sure they also know how—and when—to laugh. Tadpoles are driven to love, live, give, and laugh big. They're a blast to be with, and they inspire others to be happy. They have a work-hard, play-hard personality.

Mothers-in-law included.

DARE TO LAUGH

- Life is serious business. However, God gave us the gift of humor to help us get through even the worst of times.
- Spend time with good friends who lift your spirits and make you laugh.
- Keep an eye out for where you can inject some laughs to lighten someone else's load. In the process, your life will become lighter as well.

30

TAKING OUT THE TRASH

Tadpole Faith Finds Opportunity, Even in Garbage

I LOVE GOD'S SENSE OF humor, but sometimes He really exceeds Himself.

Like most people, I tend to make remarks on a whim—comments such as "You never know when you're going to get hit by a garbage truck" when someone expresses hesitation about buying life insurance. That's my lousy attempt to bring humor to the possibility of sudden and unexpected death. It sounds terrible, but it gets the point across, and sometimes it's closer to the truth than you would think.

One day when I stepped out of the shower, my bride let out a thunderous scream and pointed at my backside. I leaped in front of the mirror and saw nothing but purple and blue where there should have been eye-blinding natural skin color. How did I get such a wound? That's where God's sense of humor comes in.

The morning before, I'd taken the garbage out to the road to be picked up. Normally, garbage men don't pick up large items, such as broken lounge chairs, but our garbage guys are special. I've never seen them leave anything behind. I could park a broken-down school bus on cement blocks on our curb, and I'm pretty sure they would at least attempt to carry it away. I had two broken lounge chairs I wanted to toss out, but I didn't want to take advantage of our kind garbage men, so I decided to toss one away that week and the other the following week. Good plan, right?

That morning I happened to be outside when our all-star cast of garbage men came rolling down the street. I watched with bated breath to see if they would pick up the broken lounge chair. Sure enough, they tossed it in the back of the truck, and I watched as they turned on the grinding compactor, crushing it almost instantly.

I rushed out to thank the men and told them about the second chair. Would they be willing to take that one on board as well, so I didn't have to wait the extra week? Stalwart guys that they are, they told me to bring it on.

As I hustled to the back of our house to grab the second chair, the garbage truck moved to the end of our cul-de-sac to pick up our neighbors' trash. I caught up with them there, but had to drop the chair on the pavement to get a better grip on it so I could throw it in the back. I was bent over with my back to the truck, its backup warning alarm going at full blast. But by the time I heard it, it was too late for me. I did what any normal, red-blooded American would do to keep from getting run over by a thirty-two-ton mechanized behemoth only a foot away: I froze! That is, until the truck hit me right on my backside, and I went down fast and hard onto the concrete pavement. Thankfully, the truck's wheels stopped within inches of rolling on top of me.

The driver leaped out with a scream of panic. As I slowly got to my feet, I realized he was more shocked and in need of assurance than I was. The Holy Spirit, my secret weapon in life, took over. After calmly assuring him that it was my fault, not his, and that I was okay, I shared my love of Jesus Christ with him. I said I fully understood that accidents happen in life, no matter how well prepared we are. I promised him I'd already forgotten the event and told him I loved him—and I meant it.

Perhaps it was the shock of the moment that pushed me aside

long enough to let the Holy Spirit shine through. If God has to use a garbage truck to get me out of the way so He can do His work, so be it. I hope the driver thanked Jesus that I was able to walk away on that cloudy morning. I know I did. And I looked forward to more "black-and-blue" experiences with friends, family, and strangers.

The next week I gave the driver a note of encouragement and a book I believed he would enjoy reading. In a way that only God can bless us, I felt a special bond with him, and I invited him to our church. Regardless of what happens in his life through God's grace, I know for certain that he was touched in a positive way with the love of Jesus Christ. And all it took was me getting "garbed" by his garbage truck.

This incident reminds me of Satan. The moment we're not on guard, sin or garbage comes our way, and suddenly we find ourselves knocked to the ground, black and blue and wondering how we got there. Not one of us is perfect, and we all have our garbage truck moments, as evidenced in Psalm 143:3: "My enemy has chased me. He has knocked me to the ground and forces me to live in darkness like those in the grave" (NLT).

The real question is, do we stand back up after making bad choices and find the opportunities that await us? There's not a problem in the world without an opportunity specifically designed for you. Only you. The choice comes down to living a life of being bruised and blue or one that moves forward with purpose. Tadpole purpose. Psalm 143:8–10 reminds us, "Let me hear of your unfailing love each morning, for I am trusting you. Show me where to walk, for I give myself to you. Rescue me from my enemies, LORD; I run to you to hide me. Teach me to do your will, for you are my God" (NLT).

Want to live a meaningful life filled with purpose? Get in the habit of courageously standing back up when sin or the enemy knocks you down. Even if it's a thirty-two-ton truck on sixteen wheels. After all, it's only garbage, but the opportunity is priceless.

In the future I'll do a better job of getting out of the way of any massive, rolling machines coming my way. One sure thing to come out of the experience is that my garbage truck jokes have come to a complete stop.

DARE TO STAND BACK UP

- God shouldn't have to hit you with a garbage truck to get your attention, but sometimes we're that clueless and stubborn.

- Pay attention when you hear the backup warning alarms in life, and get out of the way so you're not sidelined and unable to do the tasks God has set out for you.

- Understand that God may use your misfortune to speak into the life of someone else. Your challenge could be God's megaphone.

31

ARE YOUR BRAKES ON?

Tadpole Faith Is Not a Drag

I WAS ONCE ASKED TO partner with a NASCAR driver during his off-season for a charity event at Lake Placid, New York, where the 1980 Winter Olympics were held. During the off-season, professional sports stars take a break to spend time with their families and do charity events. This event was the two-man bobsled competition, in which we competed against about ten other NASCAR teams. I was the backseat crew member, which meant I was in charge of braking around the turns. With my penchant for speed, this was a match made in heaven.

We did great during the test runs and time trials. In fact, we had the fastest practice speeds and were already marked as an easy favorite. My NASCAR driver was fearless, even though a couple of teams had just flipped their sleds on the mountainous high banks of rock-solid ice. I'd also done my part, learning how to bend my body in half to bury myself in the one-foot-by-one-foot backseat for the sake of less drag. In our final rounds, we were close to taking home the grand prize. Our times kept getting better and better. I began brushing up my victory speech for the media. We were pumped and ready to claim the gold!

When it was nearly showtime, we pushed our bright red bob-sled up to the starting gate. The green light flashed, and we were off in our Columbia- and Chevrolet-sponsored sled. With every turn, we ramped up speed as my driver kept our sled upright and moving forward. We'd already agreed that no braking would be necessary, so all I had to do was keep my nose on the floor of the sled. We were kicking ice and all-in to win.

As we crossed the finish line, I could barely contain myself. I was confident we'd broken all the records. So we were shocked to see that our time was not just slow, but slower than all of our earlier runs. Rather than setting a track record, we finished somewhere in the middle of the pack. What happened? Was the clock lying?

Our coach offered an observation that dumbfounded us both. Somehow our brake had worked itself free and slid against the ice all the way down the run without our knowing it. There was no way we could have won.

How often do we go through life not realizing our brakes are dragging? We think we're headed toward success, but pride or haste causes us to overlook something that begins to drag on our efforts. Before we realize what's happening, it's too late. My driver and I were so full of ourselves that we thought we had the race in the bag even before it began, so we didn't bother to check the brake.

The consequence for us that day at Lake Placid was merely losing a race. However, allowing pride, busyness, lust, greed, or any other sin to sneak into your life and sabotage your efforts can have far more detrimental effects. So before you set out on your next "race," don't assume you're going to win. Make sure nothing is going to hold you back. Then put your head down and prepare to hug those curves.

DARE TO CHECK THAT NOTHING IS HOLDING YOU BACK

- Don't get so caught up in winning the race that you overlook the things in your life that are slowing your progress.

- Check for any sins or vices that may be sabotaging your chances of success. God's opportunities abound every day without notice. Don't miss out!

- Celebrate your victory only after you achieve it. And don't forget to invite God to the celebration!

32

GET COMFORTABLE WITH BEING UNCOMFORTABLE

Tadpole Faith Lives Outside the Prison Cell

I ALWAYS LOVED WATCHING MY boys' baseball games when they were young. It was a time of rare pleasure, before they got older and games became more competitive—more about winning than having fun. T-ball was my all-time favorite. It was truly all about the kids and the joy of the game.

After T-ball, they graduated to coach pitching. Like any other red-blooded American dad, whenever my oldest son, Arin, was up to bat, I got a little anxious. I would often get up from my seat and walk to the fence behind home plate to get an up-close, million-dollar view.

One day I was standing at the fence behind home plate when the mother of one of my son's teammates and her six-year-old daughter walked up and stood next to me. The little girl looked at my wrist, which was at eye level for her, and then looked up at me with questioning eyes.

"What does WWJD mean?"

Yep, you got it. I wore one of those bracelets when their popularity was at its peak. I didn't know if the mother and her daughter were Christians, and the little girl's mom was already glaring at me. I struggled to come up with an answer that wouldn't offend. With a deep breath, I explained that I was a businessman and often had to make important decisions that would affect my company and my family. During those moments, I would pray and ask for Jesus' opinion, and the bracelet was a good reminder for me to do so, asking, "What would Jesus do?" in my situation.

The little girl fell silent as she pondered my answer. Her mother continued to stare at me for what seemed like an eternity, not saying a word. Then they both turned and walked away. You probably know the empty feeling you get when you think you should have said anything other than what you said.

I apologized to God for blowing it. I felt embarrassed and a little ashamed. After all, it's not every day that the Holy Spirit leads us to a near-perfect situation to be a witness for Him. I couldn't help but wonder why I hadn't been better prepared. Why didn't the Holy Spirit speak to me? Why had He left me all alone at that moment? I decided right then and there that in the future I'd leave the witnessing to the preachers and religious zealots. I had the best pity party ever. I hope God forgave me for that.

One week later I was at another one of my son's baseball games. Once again, I took up my position at the fence, unsure if the umpire could call accurate strikes and balls without me. In my peripheral vision, I noticed someone approaching from a distance of twenty feet or so. It appeared to be a woman, and her walk was brisk. With my military training, I instantly took up a defensive position.

As I turned toward her, I realized it was the mother of the little girl to whom I'd talked about my WWJD bracelet the week before. All I could think was, *God, I already apologized for not being a light for You, and now I have to take a verbal whipping from this mom?* She stood right in front of me, eye-to-eye, unsmiling. I knew the odds were in my favor of being able to duck any of her punches.

After a staring contest that seemed to last forever, she finally blurted out, "You remember last week when my daughter asked you about your WWJD bracelet? Well, the very next day, I had to take her to the Christian bookstore and buy her one too. Not only for her but also for her brother!"

I was dumbfounded. Shocked. It was the last response I'd expected.

The enemy had me convinced that taking a stand for Christ had been a waste of time. The truth of the matter is, the enemy works overtime to make us believe we're insufficient to share Christ with others. After all, that's why we have trained pastors, right? That day I learned never to be ashamed of sharing the truth with others, because not only do I have no control over how people might respond, but I also have no idea what the outcome might be. And often what I perceive as bad might turn out to be positive.

My dear friend Rita told me that one day at college she noticed an acquaintance sitting alone in the cafeteria. Rita considered sitting with her, then changed her mind for no particular reason. That night the young woman killed herself. Rita says she's always regretted not reaching out to her that day, perhaps lessening her despair by the simple act of sitting with her. But Rita couldn't have known what would happen that night; she's not God. None of us are.

In opportunities for witness, I remind myself to let my faith be bigger than my fear. Sharing Christ requires me to climb out of my comfort zone, my "prison cell," because I know God isn't interested in my comfort; he's interested in my pathway toward real growth—and being a light for others.

The truth is, Jesus doesn't *ask* us to go; He *commands* us, as His faithful followers. Is it easy? Absolutely not. But neither was jumping into a swimming pool with my hands, elbows, and feet tied together. More often than not, I hear Christians say something like, "But I don't know what to say."

Awesome! Then don't say anything. I only share whenever

the Holy Spirit speaks to my heart. And whenever God shows up, I go on automatic.

I've finally learned not to feel anxious, embarrassed, or ashamed when I tell others how God blesses me. I don't wallow in worry. *What are people going to think about me? Am I going to be asked questions to which I don't know the answers? Will I look stupid if I don't have a ready reply?* Whenever I experience such concerns, I know I'm not focusing on Jesus but on me.

Vanity can keep us in a prison cell and rob our internal joy. I love the story about the World War II Army veteran who, before his deployment overseas, found a book in a library and noticed some interesting notes in the margin. He was so intrigued that he found the name of the lady who wrote them and began writing to her. During his deployment, they became pen pals, and each letter was feathered with admiration, intrigue, and hints of a possible romance. He asked for her photo, but she refused. She felt that if he cared for her, her looks wouldn't matter.

After a year-long deployment, he returned home to New York. His heart was filled with genuine excitement to finally meet the love of his life. They agreed to meet at Grand Central Station. She told him she'd be wearing a red rose.

As he searched the crowd, he noticed a young, slim, beautiful woman dressed in a pale green suit. His heart raced with excitement. Her beauty was as fresh as springtime, and her eyes were as blue as flowers. He was overcome with so much emotion that he failed to notice that she was *not* wearing a red rose.

Flushed with disappointment as she walked past him, he saw an older, gray-haired woman who was more than plump, perhaps homeless, but proudly wearing a red rose. He attempted to hide his disappointment as he introduced himself and offered to take her to dinner, thinking that at least they could continue to be friends.

The older woman smiled sheepishly. "I don't know what's going on here," she said, "but that woman wearing the pale green suit gave me this rose and told me that if a man offered to take me to dinner, to tell him that she'd be waiting for him in the restaurant across the street. She said this was some kind of test."

We're tested every day. God wants our best. He wants us to grow, and that requires crawling outside our comfort zone and trusting Him no matter how things look at first. Tadpole faith requires us to get comfortable with being uncomfortable.

DARE TO SHARE THE TRUTH

- Every decision leads to a destination.
- No one likes to stand out as the oddball, but sometimes that's exactly what is required in order to fulfill the missions God has laid out for us.
- It may not feel comfortable initially, but we are called to sacrifice our lives for the sake of Christ, not sacrifice others for the sake of our ease.

33

THIS SIDE OF HEAVEN

Tadpole Faith Awaits Unsurpassed Celebrity Status

A SHORT WHILE AGO, MY friend Durwood Snead, who heads up international missions at one of Atlanta's megachurches, asked me to join him in Lahore, Pakistan, to do some training for pastors there. Having never been to Pakistan, I jumped at the opportunity.

En route to Lahore, Durwood and I had an extended layover in Dubai on the Persian Gulf. To treat ourselves, we arranged to spend the night at the famous Burj Al Arab, the "sailboat" hotel. It's popularly known as the world's only seven-star hotel; it's probably also the most expensive. The two-bedroom suite we'd reserved totaled 3,000 square feet—larger than many people's houses. I couldn't wait, eagerly anticipating my little slice of heaven.

When we arrived at the Dubai airport, one of the hotel staff members met us and escorted us through customs. I began to wonder if I'd been confused with some prince, but I remained mum. He helped us get our bags, then took us to meet our driver, who was waiting in a white BMW. If we'd wanted to cash in our children's college funds, we could have ridden to the hotel in one of the hotel's shining white Rolls-Royces, but the BMW was beautiful enough.

Upon arrival at the hotel, I noticed two things the moment our car door was opened at the curbside by an army of smiling servants. One was the heat—the air outside was a toasty 102°F, and that was at night. The second was that all the hotel staff greeted us by name. Apparently, the driver had called the hotel and notified them of our impending arrival. Very classy!

The heat was soon forgotten as we strolled inside and gazed at the towering fifty-six-story lobby with an illuminated aquarium on both sides of the escalators. After receiving no fewer than a dozen greetings (again by name) from the army of staff, we were escorted directly to our suite. I should say "suites" because it had several rooms, two majestic floors, and two ornate marble bathrooms.

As we settled in, the floor concierge and another gentleman came to give us a twenty-minute tour of the suite. Along with our host greeter, the concierge, the two luggage men, and the suite guide, there was a person whose sole job was to run our bathwater for us. I'm not sure how much I tipped everyone, but it certainly wasn't enough.

After everyone left, Durwood and I sat in awe for a few minutes, attempting to take in the essence of this hotel heaven. Then we realized it was already past 8:00 p.m. local time, and we hurried to pack in as many experiences as possible before having to check out at noon the following day. Like any other celebrity guest, I started by gathering up all the hotel shampoos and soaps I could find. Then, with a quick splash of cold water and fresh shirts, we were off to the gift shop. Where else can you buy a Burj Al Arab-shaped thumb drive for more than a hundred bucks? From there Durwood and I journeyed to the top floor for a nightcap.

The bar required "casual formal" dress, meaning I was obligated to change from my shower shoes and leave my baseball cap in the suite. The bar's top-floor windows offered an amazing view of other Dubai architectural wonders. The first item on the drink list was "The World's Most Expensive Drink," which went for about $8,000. Since this was our first stop on a "mission trip," I decided to hold off on that and asked instead for one of my wife's favorites, a margarita. I was too afraid to ask the price. After all, the cheapest glass of house champagne was forty dollars.

On the way back to our suite, I wondered if we should anticipate any more surprises fit for a king. I found only one: the huge multicolored marble Jacuzzi and shower with multiple heads. It was a miniature paradise. I could have snapped my fingers, and someone would have been there to run the water for me, but I chose to be adventurous as a Navy SEAL and do it on my own. I couldn't think of a more appropriate way to close out such an unforgettable evening.

As the sun came up the following day, I pressed a button, and the curtains opened along the entire east wall. The Persian Gulf was as endless as its beauty.

With only hours left until checkout, I wanted to see as much as possible. I began with a jog across the bridge along the main boulevard. Then I took a cool swim in the sculpted outdoor pool on the eighteenth floor, ideal for the weather, followed by a tour of the spa facilities. When I ventured back to the hotel for breakfast, almost the entire army of hotel staff greeted me once again by name. How could all those strangers know my name? I felt like a rock star.

After a true breakfast of champions and seemingly sincere goodbyes from the restaurant staff, I went back to the room to check on Durwood. He decided to experience the fantasy-filled breakfast buffet while I ventured outdoors on a five-minute walk to the Wild Wadi Water Park, which offered free admission to hotel guests.

If you enjoy water parks and despise the traditional long lines that tend to accompany them, Wild Wadi is the place for you. It was early, so I had a first-time teenage-like experience surfing—pretty cool for an old guy like me. Then I rode a rubber tube that worked like a roller coaster and continually sling-shot me vertically all around the water park, which left me feeling like a human lightning bolt. The best ride of the day was a waterslide with a seventy-foot vertical drop.

With our checkout time only an hour away, I hustled back to the hotel, where Durwood and I decided to make a quick trip to the indoor spa. The fine marble columns surrounding the seemingly endless pool were made for royalty.

On the way back to our room, we learned that our flight out of Dubai was delayed. Our concierge, like an angel from above, confirmed that we'd been granted a late checkout of 5:00 p.m. instead of noon. The five additional hours equated to almost a thousand dollars, but we got it at no extra charge.

For me, that meant another trip to Wild Wadi, for starters. Yes, I'm drop-dead serious. I'm a kid at heart! Then I met up with Durwood at the outdoor pool and had another opportunity to bask in cool water in the 120°F heat. It was glorious! It was also another chance for the hotel workers to line up and greet us by name.

Finally, it was time to journey back to the airport—only to realize our flight had been delayed again, so the hotel granted us another couple of hours beyond the already extended checkout time. Honestly, Durwood and I were being treated so famously, I was beginning to believe that if we had another delay, they would pay us! Those people could not stop giving. But as we know, all fantasies must come to an end.

As we finally boarded our flight to Pakistan, and I pondered the abject poverty we were about to experience, I felt a little guilty at the way we'd just indulged ourselves. However, I was also thankful to have been able to enjoy such an incredible slice of heaven right here on earth, even if only for a little while. It was a good reminder that although much of the world is in disarray, afflicted with war, famine, and disease, many other places are not.

Not only that, no matter how terrible things on this planet get, another world coexists with ours in the same way the Burj

Al Arab hotel coexists with places like Lahore. That other world is the kingdom of God, which we can experience glimpses of on earth, and which will ultimately be realized in heaven.

Once you arrive in heaven, you'll be greeted by name too. You'll be treated like a celebrity, shown to the finest suite, and have all your needs met. And it won't be a temporary stopover, forcing you to pack in every possible experience within less than a day. Nor will you have to hide away all the hotel shampoo and soaps. It will be your eternal home, a place to rest, relax, and re-cuperate before you set off on the new adventures to which God will call you.

Having had a tiny taste of such a life here on earth, I can't wait!

DARE TO ENJOY LIFE'S BLESSINGS

- Remember that the world is a balance, and while there is suffering, there is also happiness.
- God has provided glimpses of heaven throughout the world and throughout your life. Succesful warriors in battle never lose their focus, nor should any Christian.
- Don't take life so seriously that you pass up chances to experience the joy that will be ours eternally. It's a great motivation to remain faithful to the end.

34

GENTLEMEN, SAY GOODBYE
TO THE SUN

Tadpole Faith Knows It's a Masterpiece

A FEW MONTHS AGO, MIDWAY through lunch, I was asked about my Naval Special Forces past by a dear friend of mine, Dana. He wanted to know if it was true I'd been a Navy SEAL. I told him I was a graduate of BUD/S Class 89 and went to UDT 21—now SEAL Team 4 in Virginia Beach. Dana politely asked me why I never talked about it. That was easy to answer.

Anyone who talks openly about being a Navy SEAL without any prompting has likely never set foot in Coronado, California, nor graduated from BUD/S. Sadly, people who claim to be what they're not are everywhere. There's even a website dedicated to exposing fake SEALs. In fact, I met one while living in Washington, DC, when moving into a new apartment right after being discharged from the Navy.

As with any new apartment, I needed a new telephone line. The phone installer showed up and mentioned that he'd been in the Navy.

"Great!" I replied. "What did you do in the Navy?"

"I was a Navy SEAL," he said.

It wasn't his answer that triggered warning bells; it was the speed with which he responded and the fact that he did so without equivocation.

"How amazing is that!" I said, then instantly asked the million-dollar follow-up question that flushes out almost all SEAL imposters: "What BUD/S class were you in?" No real Navy SEAL would ever forget his class number.

After a few stutters and looking as if he'd been caught naked in the middle of Times Square, he confessed that he hadn't been a SEAL after all.

Events like this leave me thinking: why do so many people lie about who they are? I'm not immune to this feeling. When I first started my business, I did everything I could to make it look like a big business. Then after my business grew, I did whatever I could to make it look small and more personal, similar to the way kids try to look older, and adults try to look younger. Margaret Thatcher once said, "Being powerful is like being a lady. If you have to tell them you are, then you are not."[15]

Why do we find it so difficult to be happy with the man or woman in the mirror? As I pondered this, I realized that the only way to be content with who we are is to know *whose* we are—God's masterpiece. God tells us that even though we're all unique, we're all made in His image. We're a valued treasure, the sons and daughters of a mighty King. We were made by Him and for Him, and we're His prize! We don't have to pretend to be something we're not in order to gain acceptance from God or anyone else. All we have to do is accept our inheritance and the identity God gave us as His children, and then step into the person God created us to be.

"You are the light of the world—like a city on a hilltop that cannot be hidden. No one lights a lamp and then puts it under a basket" (Matthew 5:14–15, NLT). I can easily fall into the trap of hiding my light if I keep quiet about my faith or minimize my love for others by playing it safe and not revealing my true identity.

After all, that's safe, comfortable, and requires little or no effort on my part.

During Hell Week, once the sun had set and our night evolutions were about to begin, the Coronado gods would amuse themselves by saying, "Say goodbye to the sun, gentlemen," meaning whatever warmth and light the sun had brought during the day was now gone. The water would be colder, and our vision would be limited, especially when we ran with our boat on our heads.

One day I'll say goodbye to this earthly sun and stand before God. When that happens, I doubt He'll ask me what BUD/S class I was in, but I know I won't have to be afraid of any questions He does ask, because when it comes to God, I've never pretended to be something I'm not.

DARE TO EMBRACE WHO YOU ARE

- Don't give in to the temptation to sacrifice truth for validation from others.
- No lie can live alone, and any relationship that begins with deception is doomed to crumble and fail.
- Use truth as your foundation at all times, and your life will always be rock solid.

35

THE ONLY EASY DAY WAS YESTERDAY

Tadpole Faith Loves Being Told It Can't Do Something

IN THE FOURTH CENTURY, A monk named Telemachus felt God calling him to go to Rome. After a weeklong walk, he arrived in Rome during a huge festival. Following the roar of the crowd, he made his way to the Colosseum, where he saw gladiators standing before the Roman emperor proclaiming, "We who are about to die salute you," and then fighting each other to death, all for the entertainment of the crowds. Aghast at the pointless bloodshed, Telemachus bravely stood from the crowd and cried out, "In the name of Christ, stop!" No one paid any attention; his voice was lost in the tumult.

Undeterred, Telemachus worked his way through the teeming masses and boldly climbed down into the arena. Again he cried out, "In the name of Jesus, stop!" The crowd laughed as one of the gladiators ran him through with a sword. Telemachus's last words were, "In the name of Christ, stop!"

Then a strange thing happened. As the gladiators stood menacingly over the tiny man's body, a hush fell over the Colosseum. One spectator stood up and walked out. Then another and another. Eventually, the entire crowd left. That event took place in AD 391. Within a short time, gladiatorial fights in Rome ceased altogether.[16] All because of one man's voice.

I'm sure Telemachus was frightened. He probably didn't want to die at that moment. But isn't that exactly what Jesus calls us to do? To speak up against injustice and lay down our lives? He said there's no greater love than this (John 15:13). Telemachus didn't let his fear deter him from what God had called him to do. His obedience cost him his life, but what it gained was of far greater value.

You may not be called to speak out publicly the way Telemachus did, but perhaps you feel God calling you to speak up at work, among your friends, or in your family. Even though the stakes may not be literal life and death, the consequences of whether or not you speak up are eternal. So have no fear. There's nothing you can lose on earth for being obedient to God that He cannot restore a thousand times over in heaven.

I sometimes find myself with a group of people whose language becomes riddled with words I wouldn't want my children to hear. Or worse, I hear jokes that cross the line from clean to hurtful. Maybe you're hanging out with friends who suddenly decide to try illegal drugs or engage in some other activity that might result in arrest. The choice to speak up is always yours. Take action. You may believe you can create a new culture, and often you can. But if it doesn't work out, learn and move on. "Remember," James tells us, "it is a sin to know what you ought to do and then not do it" (James 4:17, NLT). Being available to the Holy Spirit is a full-time, 24/7 process. However, the reward is an unwavering faith that shines brightly in the darkness around you.

Every graduating BUD/S class leaves behind a gift to the Coronado gods. I'm proud to say that the gift from BUD/S Class 89 was to create a plaque with the following slogan: "The only easy day was yesterday." When you work harder every day than the day before, you become stronger, and yesterday will always seem easier than today.

I'm grateful that our Class 89 plaque still hangs in the BUD/S compound, bearing that slogan and the names of each member of our graduating class. However, I'm infinitely more grateful for our God-given ability to take a stand for Christ and fervently serve others.

Tadpole faith is never intimidated when the enemy whispers. That requires confidence, courage, and an all-in attitude. The fear of standing tall but alone while missing out on the world's approval has no hold on your heart or actions. You listen to other opinions, but you always make your own decisions.

Telemachus lost his physical life but gained eternity. Who knows how many other people his act of obedience helped to do the same? I can't wait to meet him in heaven and find out.

DARE TO SPEAK UP

- No one wants to be the lone voice calling people away from sin when it could mean getting scapegoated and attacked, but that is what Jesus calls us to do.
- Real character shines in the darkest moments. Rise above sin and live boldly.
- It may not happen immediately, but the echo of your voice speaking truth can have a radical effect on the future.
- Never underestimate the power of a single voice to change the world.

36

HIT THE SURF, PINHEADS!

Tadpole Faith Dreams Big

EVERYONE LOVES THE WONDROUS IMAGINATION of children. I've witnessed this with my four sons. I was able to take each one of them on several father-son trips, both in the United States and internationally.

When my son Evan was about six, I took him with me to Washington, DC. I will never forget the stunned look on his six-year-old face when he first saw the Lincoln Memorial. Evan loves to talk, so whenever he's silent, I know something's going on inside his fast-thinking head. After climbing the many steps of the memorial, Evan gazed silently at the nineteen-foot-tall statue of Lincoln. It was one of those rare moments when he was speechless. Not a word.

Finally, with his eyes like saucers, he turned to me and said, "Wow, Dad, I had no idea Abe Lincoln was such a big guy!" I couldn't help but laugh.

On another occasion, we were in an athletic shoe store that had a large circular running track inside. It was a perfect place for little kids to give their new running shoes a test spin. After Evan had picked out his shoes, I told him to take a few laps, saying I was sure he would fly in his new runners. He didn't hesitate, and did he ever run!

On the first lap, I saw nothing but pure grit written all over his face. On lap two, he showed even more determination. By lap three, I noticed a touch of disappointment. By lap four, he was almost crying.

Thinking that he'd pulled a muscle or something worse, I ran over and asked him what was wrong. He looked at me with the saddest expression I've ever seen. "Dad, I did my best," he said, "but I still couldn't fly."

Once again, I couldn't hold back my laughter, but it also made me think: at what point do we lose the ability to think over the top, to dream bigger than life, to embrace the power of our words, to imagine that we can achieve the impossible? I wonder how often God is waiting for us to take Him at His Word. Maybe He *does* want us to fly instead of just run around in circles.

Like a child, all we have to do is believe. Dream bigger. Didn't Jesus tell us this very thing? "Very truly I tell you, whoever believes in me will do the works I have been doing, and they will do even greater things than these, because I am going to the Father" (John 14:12, NIV).

Author Kenneth Hildebrand writes, "The poorest of men is not the one without a nickel to his name. He is the fellow without a dream .. a great ship made for the mighty ocean but trying to navigate in a millpond. He has no far port to reach, no lifting horizon, no precious cargo to carry. His hours are absorbed in routine and petty tyrannies."[17]

Any worthwhile dream will require risk and sacrifice. And that's a good thing. Robert Orben says, "Always remember that there are two types of people in this world, the realists and the dreamers. The realists know where they're going. The dreamers have already been there."[18]

Whenever we tadpoles did something wrong, the Coronado gods would shout, "Hit the surf, pinheads!" Even today, I often have to "hit the surf" to get out of God's way and watch Him do His thing—which is always bigger than anything I might have in mind. When I do step aside, God comes through. And then, like Evan looking up at the statue of Abraham Lincoln, I stand there, awestruck. "I didn't realize God was so big!"

Will I ever learn?

DARE TO DREAM BIG

- God calls us to be like little children, which means dreaming like children. You're wired by the Creator of Heaven and the universe; prepare for infinitely more.

- If we don't dream big, that's a guarantee that nothing extraordinary will happen.

- Circumstances may not always turn out the way we want, but that is beyond our control. Set goals, be 100 percent in, and be action-oriented.

37

WHERE'S WALDO?

Tadpole Faith Never Buys into the "You're All Alone" Lie

WHEN MY BOYS WERE TODDLERS, we enjoyed the *Where's Waldo?* books. The pages in these children's books are filled with intricately detailed images, and hidden somewhere in each picture was Waldo, a guy in a red-and-white shirt, matching stocking cap, and blue pants. Finding Waldo required a careful eye and enduring patience. My boys loved it, and I enjoyed competing with them to see who could find Waldo first. Sometimes we were tempted to give up. Had the artist forgotten to put Waldo on that page? But we kept looking, and eventually we found him.

One day while reflecting on the fun we used to have, I thought about how finding Waldo is a lot like finding Jesus. Sometimes life becomes so complicated and stressful that we can't see Jesus anywhere. We yearn for His familiar, comforting, smiling face, but all we find is messiness and noise. As Christians we know that Jesus has promised never to leave us or forsake us. That means no matter what we're going through, Jesus is there. We need to open our eyes, be patient, and keep looking until we find Him.

The same goes for traumatic events from your past. Jesus didn't abandon you in those moments, even though it might have felt that way. He was right there with you, suffering as you suffered, experiencing everything you experienced. He loves you, He created you, and He lives in you. If you can't see Him as you reflect on those past events, keep looking, because I guarantee He was there. "The LORD is good, a stronghold in the day of trouble; he knows those who take refuge in him" (Nahum 1:7, ESV).

Finding Jesus in those moments can bring you an incredible amount of healing and peace. It should also give you confidence the next time you go through a trial because rather than focusing on the problem, you can keep your eyes peeled for Jesus. Like Waldo, He's always somewhere in the picture. You just need to have your heart open and the unabashed perseverance to look until you find Him.

DARE TO FIND JESUS

- People often wonder where God is, especially in the darkest of times. However, if you keep your eye out for Him, you will find Jesus in the most unlikely places.
- Jesus loves you, and He suffers with you when you are suffering.
- Even in the midst of your darkest pain, He's right there beside you.
- Don't dare let any suffering be wasted. May we be worthy.

38

THE THORN

Tadpole Faith Does This When Life Is Unbearable

MIDMORNING ON SEPTEMBER 29, 2015, I was in my office answering emails when my second-oldest son, Evan, raced in screaming hysterically and shouting for me to follow him into his bedroom. When we got there, I found my twenty-year-old son, Chris, crumpled on the floor, unconscious.

We called 911 and began administering CPR, as did the paramedics when they arrived. But it was all for naught. Chris died at the hospital a short time later. Having wrestled with depression for some time, his struggle was finally over. For the rest of our family, the battle was just beginning.

As I moved through the shock and began the grieving process, I started to research the topic of suicide. I realized we were far from alone in our grief. In the most recent available annual statistics, according to the Centers for Disease Control and Prevention, there were 47,500 deaths by suicide in the United States. Suicide is the tenth most common cause of death in our country. Most alarming, it's the second most common cause of death for people ages ten to thirty-four. At that time, approximately 130 Americans died each day by suicide. That equated to one suicide death in the United States every eleven minutes.[19]

The family members, close friends, and other people who care most about the person who commits suicide will never be the same. It's been said that each suicide dramatically affects the lives of six to ten people. I've also seen reports that say the number is as high as sixteen.

When someone close to you takes his or her life, questions linger. Voices in your head ask, "What if I'd done this or that?" At different points, survivors feel shock, guilt, shame, depression, pain, and loss. It's a fertile field for Satan, who thrives on burdening people with feelings of hopelessness, despair, and sorrow. Through it all echoes the lingering question: "Why?" Even if we knew the answer, it wouldn't change the outcome.

Though all deaths are painful, death by suicide stings the heart like no other. Depression lingers outside your door calling your name and the names of your family members. Friends and family rarely discuss suicide deaths. It's forbidden ground, a painfully deep wound that never heals. Even close family members feel awkward, not knowing what to say, so most say nothing at all. No words seem necessary when people look at you with tears in their eyes.

Just yesterday at church, the worship band sang "Oceans" by Hillsong United. Although it's been a while now, I gave it my all to sing those lyrics, but no words would come out. My eyes teared up. I couldn't sing because my heart was overwhelmed with pain. Raw. All I could do was focus on the words: "Lord, take me deeper than my feet could ever wander, and my faith will be made stronger."[20]

Someone close to our son's situation said that I must hate God. My response was, "No, I hate sin."

Satan is the father of all lies, and despair is his signature. How does Jesus tell us to handle grief? He says we must use our pain for ministry. If we want to live for others, we must never allow our sorrow to turn into self-pity or self-loathing.

Since Chris's death, my faith isn't weaker; it's stronger and purer. That may sound strange, but I feel God listening to me as I eagerly listen to Him. I never have to think about walking to the cross because I never leave it. The foot of the cross is my home. This is where I breathe. No matter where I am or where I go, He's with me, and I'm with Him, seeking oneness. Now I can totally acknowledge that each breath comes from Him. Deb and I love others in a unique way, far different from before. The little things that people do for others cause our tears to well up instantly.

In business or at home, if I ever become proud of any accomplishments, all I have to do is get into my car and travel fifteen minutes to Chris's grave, where I'm reminded instantly that this life is temporary. It's not my life that matters, but how I live for God, how I go beyond my comfort zone and live for others.

Remember when Jesus was told about the death of John the Baptist? What did Jesus do? We find out in Matthew 14. First, He slipped away in a boat to be alone. I believe it's safe to say that He prayed. Upon His return to shore, He immediately began to heal the sick. A short time afterward, on that same day, He fed 5,000 people with 5 loaves of bread and 2 fish. Then, hours later, He reassured His disciples by calming a frantic storm while walking out to them on the water. All within twenty-four hours of John the Baptist's death. Jesus' actions that day reflect the words of Psalm 107:28–31: "Then they cried out to the LORD in their trouble, and he brought them out of their distress. He stilled the storm to a whisper; the waves of the sea were hushed. They were glad when it grew calm, and he guided them to their desired haven" (NIV). Jesus had a mission that day (as every day), and that mission was bigger than His sorrow.

Yes, I know He was Jesus Christ, God in the flesh. But aren't we called to be imitators of Christ? Regardless of life's circumstances, however painful, our mission remains. When confronted by divorce, loss of a loved one, or any of the other destructive storms life throws our way, we require a season of heartfelt prayer. Then, following Jesus' example, we're to move beyond grief and channel our sorrow into something positive, active, and life-giving for ourselves and the people around us. If you're hurting, it's unlikely you're the only one. So do what you can to help bear another's burden.

There's a season for all things—a time to grieve, a time to pray, and a time to resume our mission, just like Jesus. The more time I spend trying to be like Jesus, even in the midst of pain, the easier it is to find hope.

The most helpful thing in the immediate aftermath of Chris's suicide was prayer. I would pray on my knees and then lie in bed continuing to talk with Jesus. Nonstop. In the midst of my pain, God listened. Whenever that dark cloud began hovering over me, like a child I went straight to Jesus, just as Jesus went to His Father.

Just as important, I kept God's Word close by. I surrounded myself with Scripture, especially the Psalms. Mornings were the best for me since clarity seems to fade through the course of the day. His Word filled my tank whenever I was in need. I couldn't stand or breathe outside of God's presence. I clung to Jesus through constant prayer and by diving into His Word. Without fervent prayer and getting deep into God's Word during those moments of overwhelming grief, I'm not sure I would have survived. I even found comfort gripping my Bible while resting in bed.

In addition to prayer and reading Scripture, I kept a journal. It's amazing to look at all the experiences, thoughts, and prayers I managed to record, tracking my progress through various stages of dealing with Chris's death. And the process is far from over.

When the pain feels as if it's too great to move forward, I stop and weep. But only for a season. Then I go to my knees. One doesn't happen without the other. I've found that the deeper the weeping, the deeper the feeling of physical comfort I feel afterward. It's amazing how God created and prepared our bodies to overcome all sorts of struggles, provided we truly trust Him.

No matter the circumstances, God created you for a purpose,

His purpose. Do you want to fulfill that purpose? Then follow Jesus. Move through your grief with meaningful prayer. Walk in Jesus' footsteps rather than in your emotions. Stand on solid ground instead of shifting sand. When God reveals that it's time to grow beyond your comfort and be others-focused, go full throttle. Don't look back; keep your gaze on Jesus. Keep moving.

Don't give the enemy a foothold in your grief. The pit of despair is dark and profound. You cannot be like Christ and drown in self-pity at the same time. Your value, purpose, and significance are anchored not in your circumstances but in God. In God's timing, this becomes more evident as your recovery from grief progresses, and as you lean into Jesus along the way.

Remember, God wants you to live a life full of joy. Without such joy, how can you offer anyone good news, especially God's good news? By being a light in a dark world, you can send the shadows back where they belong.

My goal is for my sorrow to propel me to love and serve others. Yes, Satan is a powerful enemy, and he may have won the short-term battle for Chris's life, but he won't win the battle for mine. All this sorrow that the enemy intended to be used for evil will be used for good instead. Chris's life has become my anthem for loving and serving others while exposing Satan's lies, which blind us and lead us down dark paths. With Jesus, I don't stand alone, and I'm not afraid. My faith is bigger than my fear.

Through my brokenness, I find Jesus; I have to. He gives me purpose, and His purpose is always good. Every day I remind myself that God either makes things happen or allows them to happen. Not only that, but all things, even death, work together for the good of those who love God. Such thoughts help me experience God's love and grace. Each experience shows me His purpose and direction in my life. No matter how dire the circumstances, they're always inversely proportional to the good that God can create through His infinite wisdom. But believing this requires real trust.

Are you in the midst of a storm? Feeling like giving up? Struggling to find purpose in life? Is the pain too overwhelming? Does sorrow fill your every waking moment?

I understand; I really do. But don't you dare give up and let the enemy win. Follow Jesus' example. Discover trust on a whole new level. Find oneness in him. Find the good in all circumstances, even death.

Sometimes the worst roads lead to the most beautiful places. It's a choice. Perhaps the toughest choice a person can imagine. Meanwhile, your God-given purpose never sleeps.

DARE TO TURN TO GOD IN GRIEF

- We can allow our grief to suck us down into a deep, dark hole, or we can use it as a tool to draw closer to God and each other.
- If you are struggling with grief, seek God through prayer and God's Word.
- God will never abandon you. Never.

39

LOSING—AND FINDING— MYSELF IN MY CHURCH COMMUNITY

Tadpole Faith Accepts Support

FOR ME, HAVING A CHURCH to call home was like finding oxygen. Many people think of church as a building or denomination. The word *church* in the New Testament translates the Greek word *ekklesia*, which means "the called-out ones"—in this case, a body of Christ followers. That really mattered to Deb and me in the wake of Chris's death. The pain of a child's suicide leaves you grasping for a purpose, even asking yourself, "Why go on?"

Chris died just before noon on a cloudy Tuesday. Within minutes people began rushing to our home, entering without knocking. At a time like that, doorbells are unnecessary. With a single call to Chris Boynton, one of our awesome student group leaders at Passion City Church, friends began arriving from around the city. To this day, I have no idea how they showed up so quickly.

Before long about ten of the church's student group leaders were surrounding and supporting our son Avery. Two of the leaders even drove out to his high school where he was a senior and waited by Avery's car to ensure he wouldn't have to drive home alone that day, although it was only a five-minute ride. It was a great example of a battle-ready, Christ-modeled church acting in real time.

Just after Chris's death, life was nothing more than a deafening shockwave. I was numb to all feeling. I tried to look and act normal, but in reality I felt empty and breathless. Living another day made little sense. On the verge of collapse, I felt Satan turn up the volume in my mind.

Robertson Davies wrote, "Extraordinary people survive under the most terrible circumstances and then become even more extraordinary because of it."[21] Yes, but I wanted absolutely nothing to do with extraordinary. I would have preferred to die right there, right then—if only God would call me home.

The day after Chris's death, we had to begin making funeral arrangements, painful though it was. Along with Sandy, our dearest friend, Debbie and I visited a highly recommended funeral home. We toured the chapel for Chris's memorial service, then selected a gravesite on top of a hill. After signing all the documents, we left the funeral home office. Then, right there in the parking lot, Debbie broke down in tears.

"This doesn't feel right," she said, explaining that the chapel was too traditional for a contemporary and free-spirited kid like Chris. Also, we could see the roof of the funeral home from his gravesite, and Chris hated funeral homes; he would hold his breath whenever he passed one. I know, it was irrational, but weary emotions aren't lucid.

As I attempted to comfort Debbie, I became overwhelmed with all the collective emotions and the short timeline. I began to panic, feeling the ground rushing toward me.

I tracked down the funeral home director and told him to put everything on hold. He politely acknowledged our concerns and gave us another tour of the cemetery, so we could choose another gravesite. We didn't see anything we liked. Then we took a third tour by ourselves and, surprisingly, found a site that overlooked a small lake and was close to a stand of trees. We all agreed that was the place. In fact, Deb and I purchased the plot next to Chris so he wouldn't be alone. Yes, we knew we were burying only his body, but we were too drained to battle reason. All I can say is, it feels good to know that our bodies will be together forever.

We returned home to find cars lining the street, people inside and outside our home, and dinner being prepared in our kitchen for everyone. Our friends had abandoned their vacations and taken time off from work to love us and grieve with us.

Over the following days, people continued to visit, bringing food, grieving with us, but mostly loving us. Our front door was never locked. Our *ekklesia*, our church, seemed to never take their eyes off Debbie and me. They cared for, loved, and strived to protect us as if we were newborns. One of our dear pastors, Brad Jones, continued to call, text, visit, and do whatever was necessary to ensure we knew we were prayed for and loved. No limits. No boundaries for such relentless love. This too was the church.

When Thursday morning arrived, the final funeral plans hadn't yet been made. We knew only that the funeral should be on Saturday since out-of-town guests had to be back at work on Monday. Debbie and I agreed on a graveside service, where people could share memories of Chris. Instead of a formal memorial service, we would just keep our home open to anyone who wanted to share their love, thoughts, and prayers—a continuation of what had been occurring spontaneously. Our front door would remain unlocked. It was an awesome plan. Or so I thought.

I texted Pastor Brad to let him know our decision, only to discover he was on his way to our home. When he arrived we told him our plans to have only a graveside service. Brad, who has a Mount Everest–size heart, was both gentle and firm in his response. "Larry," he said, "I feel very strongly that the church needs to love on and pray over you and Debbie. We'll take care of everything."

I had nothing left in my tank, so I didn't argue. Brad suggested a reception provided by Passion City Church at our home immediately following the graveside service. I agreed, with one stipulation. Since our two oldest sons were angry with God and promised to walk away from the graveside service if there was any "Bible talk," I insisted that praise and worship take place only during the reception.

On Friday, food continued to show up at our front door. Out-of-town family members had been arriving throughout the night. The coffeepot became mobile, as early morning coffee drinkers didn't want to wake up guests sleeping near the kitchen. They congregated everywhere, from our master bath to the laundry room. Our home turned into a mega center for loving compassion, just like church.

Saturday quickly arrived. The graveside service was to take place at 10:00 a.m. I had no idea how the day would end. The best I could do was pray my way from one moment to the next. It gave an entirely new meaning to the term Hell Week. I was on automatic. I told the Lord this was His day, not mine. Out-of-town family continued to arrive at our home up to the final hour before we departed for the graveside service. We all had one hope in common: to hold it together for the next few hours, at least on the outside.

The graveside service was for family and close personal friends only. Eighty or so people were with us. Pastor Brad led the service like an angel sent from heaven. Maybe he was. For a full hour and a half, friends and family shared stories about Chris. Many of their memories were funny ones. Almost all were endearing. Each was a special memory that will never be forgotten. This I surely believe: Chris touched more lives than he realized.

As we arrived home, we were shocked to see several of the surrounding streets overflowing with parked cars. In the sweeping rain, men from our church stood up and down the streets guiding traffic and escorting people under their umbrellas. I'd never seen both of the double front doors of our house open before that day. It was so welcoming, so like church!

Indeed, the church took over. More than two dozen Passion City lovers of Christ loved and served our family, friends, and anyone else who walked through those two huge front doors that day. They served food and saw that no need went unmet or over-looked. It was so like Jesus. I'd never attended such a Saturday gathering in a home until that day. It was as if the early church had come back to life.

Pastor Brad breathed life into our home with his opening words.

Worship leader Todd Fields welcomed the Holy Spirit with his songs of worship.

Pastor Louie Giglio shared that during times of uncertainty, we must cling to the one thing that's certain: Jesus. His Spirit-filled words assured Deb and me that Jesus understood exactly what we were feeling, and he promised that Jesus wasn't done writing the Fowler story. Louie proclaimed, "Our circumstances don't frame our view of God; rather, Jesus frames our view of our cir-cumstances. The Holy Spirit is not finished yet."

Chris Boynton spoke directly to Avery, assuring him that he would not be walking through this alone. His words were so heart-felt, so important for a younger brother to hear at a time like that.

Although no calls for salvation were offered, seeds were planted. Some surely fell on the footpath and some on rocks, but hopefully, none were left among the thorns. I'm confident that precious seeds were planted in good soil that day.

A friend shared a powerful truth with Debbie and me: "Your capacity for compassion, comfort, and connection are multiplied from your great conflict and loss." As Christians, we try to be prepared for the storms in life, because they'll surely come. On our own, we can't succeed, but God never abandons us. Neither will His church, not even in the midst of the all-powerful sting of death. With lasting faith, we won't turn our backs and flee but boldly turn our faces into the storm and proclaim that we are His.

As we learned more than ever on that day, the church is not

a building. It's Christ and His followers, who choose to love through action. Such a church of called-out people binds us to Jesus. The church imitates Jesus and pronounces the secret of having true joy and lasting peace, even in the darkest of moments. The church is fearless. It's active.

In the movie *Black Hawk Down,* a vehicle filled with shot-up American soldiers comes to a stop in the middle of a street where Somali bullets are flying everywhere. The officer in charge (OIC) tells a soldier to get in and start driving.

"I can't!" the soldier yells. "I'm shot!"

"We're all shot," the OIC replies. "Get in and drive!"

I'm sure many of the people who loved on us that day were also "all shot," deep in the midst of their own struggles, but they set that aside and served us anyway. This is the church, a stirring community of Jesus followers who serve despite—and because of—their wounds.

If you haven't found a church, don't give up. Get in and drive. If you're in the middle of a storm, don't give up. Get in and drive. God and His people await you with the love that no words or tears can ever explain while on earth.

DARE TO RELY ON YOUR CHURCH

- People find lots of things to criticize about the church. However, when disaster strikes, nothing is more powerful or reassuring than being enfolded in the body of Christ.

- The church is a present-day practice of the eternal reality we will experience after death.

- If you haven't found a church where you feel at home, know that it is out there and worth the effort to find. And remember, no church is perfect: major on the majors and minor on the minors.

- People who have suffered naturally expose a maturity that cannot be taught. Such maturity enables boundless compassion for others suffering similarly.

40

IT MAY NOT PAY TO BE A WINNER

Tadpole Faith Is Never Too Proud

AS A CHILD, I AVOIDED graveyards. I guess the thought of buried bodies decomposing made me uncomfortable.

Things have changed.

At least once a week, and usually two or three times, I pack up my red University of Georgia football folding chair, some reading material (including my Bible), pens, flowers, something new to leave on Chris's headstone, my Lauren Daigle playlist and headphones, and on hot days a couple bottles of water to give to the mighty men who oversee the graveyard. I spend anywhere from twenty minutes to three hours there.

I know you're likely thinking, *Why?* After all, if I'm a Christian, as I claim to be, don't I believe Chris is in heaven? Of course I do! But somehow, whenever I'm alone there, I find it easy to talk with God. Don't think I'm nuts, but many times He replies. The graveside gives me quiet time like no other. The fresh breeze, the beauty of God's natural kingdom, and no interruptions. I feel as if I have God's full attention. And He certainly has mine.

At times as I sit there at Chris's grave overlooking a calm lake that's perfectly placed, I reflect on my time as a Navy Special Forces operator—and on one memory in particular. During our first week in BUD/S, 200 men with shaved heads gathered around for a team meeting. Our class proctor, Mr. Twidek, led the discussion. It was his job to nurture us along the best he could and also to answer our questions about how to survive BUD/S. His encouragement was similar to that of a protective parent but without the embrace—he was a Navy SEAL, after all. But he was on our side and did his best to lift our spirits during low times. Those low moments occurred when training became unbearable and fellow trainees rang out and quit.

At that first team meeting, Mr. Twidek made an off-the-cuff comment I'll never forget. "If you graduate BUD/S, you'll have life by the balls." Those words stuck with me through many trials and storms. Graduating from BUD/S and moving onward with the teams made me believe that statement even more. I've received blows to the head and been knocked down too many times to count. But I had the perseverance of a Navy SEAL, and I knew it wasn't just getting back up that counted, but *jumping* back up and begging for more. That attitude gave me the survival skills of a mountain lion.

Until September 29, 2015—the day Chris took his life.

When I sit a few feet from my son's grave, God reminds me that despite everything I've achieved, I certainly don't have life by the balls. Sure, there are moments when I can stand tall, but the foundation of those proud moments is nothing more than sand— firm during low tide, but becoming looser and shifting more with each relentless wave.

When things are going well, it's human nature to lower our guard and assume we finally have this "life" thing all figured out. However, that's usually right about the time the tables turn, and we find ourselves struggling and confused, wondering what went wrong.

Our BUD/S Class 89 motto, "The only easy day was yester-day," has become synonymous with the Navy SEALs. I've learned the truth of those words over and over. Just when you think you have life by the balls, suddenly you feel a tight, uncomfortable grip on your nether regions, and you realize the tables have turned.

Each time I visit Chris's grave, I pray and listen to what God has to say, and He always helps me put my worldly successes and failures into proper perspective. I've learned not to be surprised whenever God speaks. At those times, life seems to make sense— if only for a moment. I don't need to be at Chris's graveside any longer for that to happen, but it's amazing how quickly being there helps me refocus on what's most important.

If you feel proud or feel like you've conquered the world and now have life by the balls, you're actually in a dangerous position. Rather than assume you have things all sorted out, even when you experience great success, stick close to God, and remain hum-ble, because you'll be amazed at how quickly circumstances can deteriorate.

DARE TO BE HUMBLE

- Just because today was easy doesn't mean tomorrow will be.
- Don't coast on yesterday's successes.
- Remember that each challenge prepares us for an even bigger one to come.

41

THE LURE OF A LOW PROFILE

Tadpole Faith Is Not Remembered by Silence

I MENTIONED EARLIER THE TADPOLES' unspoken rule of the road about staying in the middle of the pack. Sometimes during the bootstrapped beach runs, a four-wheel pickup truck with a loudspeaker attached would follow alongside the slow runners; the occupants were blasting constant, repetitive sarcastic insults, calling out people by name at what seemed like 120 decibels. They caused the inner soul to vibrate with the overpowering urge to quit and be done with the pain and scathing tirades.

To survive BUD/S and reduce the risk of revved-up harassment from the Coronado gods, it seemed crucial not to attract special attention—either by being pridefully out in front of the team (and thereby inflating the gods' expectations of our future performance to unattainable levels) or even worse, lagging behind. The goal was to remain low profile. The gods could not abuse what they could not see—at least in theory.

Today as a Christ follower, I often find myself instinctively choosing a low profile. I'm not alone. I've heard it referred to as "country club Christianity," living within one's comfort zone. I call it a "low-profile faith"—holding back and remaining in the middle . . not living to the max the life for which God created me.

My dear friend Roger, who runs a highly successful business, offered his testimony to a group of his golfing buddies one night at his home. He spoke about his life as a husband, as a father, and finally, as a Christian. Afterward, one of his guests mentioned that in all his years of knowing him, he never suspected that Roger was a Christian too. That comment changed Roger's life. He wants others to know about his faith.

Many Christians live a low-profile life in regard to their faith. Reasons range from being politically correct in the office to not knowing what to say. Excuses abound. Many of us fail to regularly open the Scriptures to hear what God has to say to us. We may feel unequipped to share the good news. For a few, we tend to believe that sharing the gospel is the pastor's work. For the rest of us, attending church once a week feels like an ample fulfillment of our role in the great commission.

The Scriptures are pretty direct in terms of warning against sustained quietness about our faith or striving to stay politically correct. Check out these verses: "Preach the word; be ready in season and out of season; reprove, rebuke, and exhort, with complete patience and teaching" (2 Timothy 4:2, ESV). "Take no part in the unfruitful works of darkness, but instead expose them" (Ephesians 5:11, ESV). Tadpole faith isn't predicated on the opinions or fears of others or on whatever is politically correct for the day. It's founded exclusively on God's Word.

Sadly, Satan has twisted the minds of many and influenced them to remain silent about biblical principles concerning issues such as abortion. They even ignore God's command to expose sin like abusive anger, laziness, pridefulness, anxiety, and sexual immorality. Denouncing sin is never denouncing the person committing the sin. The world loudly protests that the Bible's teachings equate to hatred and go against the world's standards of acceptance and tolerance. In truth, Satan is winning over the majority in America as believers remain quiet. Even church leaders rarely speak out against sensitive social issues that go against biblical truths. They act as if the church's highest priority is to not offend anyone or not to be labeled as intolerant.

Although living in different circumstances, in 1965, Martin Luther King Jr. spoke about the results of maintaining a low profile: "History will have to record the greatest tragedy of this period of social transition was not the vitriolic words and other violent actions of the bad people but the appalling silence and indifference of the good people. Our generation will have to repent not only the words and acts of the children of darkness but also for the fears and apathy of the children of light." King added, "In the end, we will remember not the words of our enemies, but the silence of our friends."[22] The same problem of low-profile faith that King observed during the civil rights movement is with us today. The enemy remains. One of his primary weapons is intimidation through worldly opinions.

But one thing is certain: Christian men and women throughout history have bravely and boldly lived out their faith and will forever be remembered for not maintaining a low profile. William Wilberforce risked his career in his effort to abolish slavery in the British Empire. Dietrich Bonhoeffer was imprisoned and killed for opposing the Nazis in Germany. Jim Elliot, along with four other missionaries, was killed on January 8, 1956, while trying to bring the gospel to the Auca people of Ecuador. Not to be beaten by the enemy, their widows later made peaceful contact with the tribe and shared Christ with the man who took Elliot's life. This murderer became a Christ follower.

Tadpole faith is never silent. It is not intimidated by the enemy's whispers. The fear of not being in step with the world's view has no hold on your heart. We're called to trust God without any fear, especially of the world's opinion.

Famed atheist comedian Penn Jillette once said this about Christianity: "I don't respect people who don't proselytize. I don't respect that at all. If you believe that there is a heaven and hell and people could be going to hell or not getting eternal life or whatever, and you think that it's not worth telling them this because it would make it socially awkward . . How much do you have to hate somebody to believe that everlasting life is possible and not tell them that?"[23]

Tadpole faith is all about making life count. This kind of commitment and daring focus doesn't waver with the wind. Those with tadpole faith reflect a light that is unmistakable, no matter the evil lurking in the dark.

Jesus said, "Anyone who isn't with me opposes me, and anyone who isn't working with me is working against me" (Matthew 12:30, NLT). How then can it even be possible to live a low-profile Christian life and still be following Jesus? Jesus could have lived a low-profile life during His ministry, but He chose the pain of being nailed to the cross for you and me instead.

We get to choose what kind of faith we're going to live every day. Tadpole faith is constant, bold, and focused. It is centered not on self but on God's power and living in dependence on that power with all of one's mind, body, and soul.

That kind of faith is never looking for the middle of the pack. It always runs to win.

DARE TO BE LOUD

- It's tempting to keep our heads down and stay out of trouble, not speaking out or acting in ways that differentiate us from the group. However, that's exactly what Jesus has called us not to do.
- There's nothing low profile about the Christian life.
- The minute you agree to follow Jesus, you are agreeing to stand out, no matter the consequences.

42

CURSE OR BLESSING?

Tadpole Faith Is Worthy of Suffering

FAITH IS WHAT PROVIDES THE confidence to succeed. However, it's costly—as anything worthwhile is. Life's journeys are never perfect, nor should they be. The obstacles life brings are brutal. Sometimes you may feel like you're living through Hell Week over and over. Faith allows us to face imperfections and required sacrifices with courage.

On September 29, 2017—two years to the day after our son Chris died—hope was a distant thought. Deb and I sat inside the office of an oncologist and heard him utter words no one ever wants to hear: "You have cancer." Not just any cancer, but non-Hodgkin's lymphoma, which had manifested in a tumor the size of a cantaloupe painfully fighting for the same space as my abdomen. I knew at that moment my life would never be the same.

The next few days were a blur. What I remember clearly is the pain, due in part to the size of the tumor. The days were filled with surgeries and tests to determine whether my body could handle the dreaded chemo.

Illness, injury, love, lost moments of true greatness, and sheer stupidity all occur to test the boundaries of our souls. Without such tests, life would be a straight, flat road to nowhere. It would be safe and comfortable, but it would also be dull and utterly pointless. Throughout anyone's journey, things will happen that will seem horrible, painful, and unfair. But those moments come with a blessing. Without overcoming such obstacles, you will never realize your full potential, strength, willpower, or heart. As I thought through my previous battles, I fell to my knees and began thanking the Lord in advance for each and every day to come.

Victor's Frankl's book *Man's Search for Meaning* explores how life holds potential meaning in the most horrific circumstances. Frankl shares his experiences in the Auschwitz concentration camp, where ninety percent of the new arrivals were gassed within the first few hours, while others slowly starved to death. More than six million people died during the Holocaust. Frankl wrote of his time in Auschwitz, "When the last layers of subcutaneous fat had vanished, and we looked like skeletons disguised with skin and rags, we could watch our bodies beginning to devour themselves."[24]

He went on to say that even in the concentration camps, some men walked through the huts comforting others, giving away their last piece of bread. One man hid a crumb in his armpit to give to another more in need. They may have been few in number, but men at their worst and near death still maintained the freedom to choose their meaning and purpose.

Viktor Frankl also tells the story of a young woman he met at Auschwitz who was on the brink of death. Despite her situation, she was cheerful and upbeat. "I am grateful that fate has hit me so hard," she confessed. "In my former life, I was spoiled and did not take spiritual accomplishments seriously." As she was talking, she looked out the window of the concentration camp hut. "This tree here is the only friend I have in my loneliness, and I often talk to this tree." Frankl was startled and didn't know how to respond, being concerned that she was delirious and hallucinating. When he boldly asked her if the tree ever replied, she said, "Yes, it said to me, I am here—I am."

The concentration camp survivors proved that their last inner freedom could not be taken away. It can be said that they were worthy of their sufferings. The way they bore pain was a genuine achievement. It's this spiritual freedom—which cannot be taken away—that makes life meaningful and purposeful.

Life is a mess. Humans have flaws. Things happen. Broken relationships, business failures, cancer, and even death seem horrible and may lead us to think, *Why go on?* In these moments, we must search for the courage and perseverance that will exceed such pain.

But can we always find purpose in the pain?

Rick Warren may have expressed it best: "If you want God to bless you and use you greatly, you must be willing to walk with a limp for the rest of your life, because God uses weak people."[25] Without painful obstacles, a reason to limp, we'll never come to realize our deeply anchored courage, wisdom, and confidence. The great Russian novelist Fyodor Dostoevsky said, "Pain and suffering are always inevitable for a large intelligence and a deep heart. The really great men must, I think, have great sadness on earth."

The secret of every Hell Week survivor who went on to become a SEAL is that they understood the meaning of never giving up. Hurdles were made for leaping over, not to serve as roadblocks. A SEAL continues moving forward no matter the pain. As author Nicky Verd has said, "Pain is meant to produce purpose, not to kill it."[26]

Like tadpoles in the sewage-infested Tijuana mudflats, there are moments in life when we're called to rise and overcome—not through our own strength but by surrendering to Jesus, our perfect example of how to overcome life's adversities and be transformed in the process. Who knows? Maybe your life's purpose is to be a witness for others through your trials. Rick Warren explained, "Experience is not what happens to you. It is what you do with what happens to you. Don't waste your pain; use it to help others."[27] I know pain can seem all-consuming, but it's not about us; it's about him. During life's tragic moments, the enemy and his minions may swarm all over us like hungry vultures; but as we embrace Christ, we need never allow such sorrows to go to waste.

As I said earlier in this book, if you're not currently in adversity, then look out, because adversity's on the way. Whether as a Navy SEAL, in business, or in my family and personal relationships, adversity has purified my heart like gold in a crucible. In the midst of trials, I know I'm never alone. Instead of lamenting my situation, I seek oneness with my heavenly Father. I feel Him listening to my prayers. We talk constantly. He's my refuge and my strength. No trial is wasted. No matter how bad my circumstances, I always step back and seek a redeeming purpose because I know God wins every time.

In 2 Corinthians 12:7, the apostle Paul mentions being given "a thorn in my flesh, a messenger of Satan, to torment me" (NIV). I know what it is to have a thorn in my flesh. Such a thorn eliminates fleeting thoughts of pride and fuels my hatred of sin. Above all, it reminds me of my weakness and my utter dependence on God.

Christ showed us there's a season for everything, including grief, but we're not to stay there. As painful as grieving is, it should not subvert our identity in Christ. That subversion is the enemy's objective, so remain vigilant in employing the two-second rule. Don't allow negative thoughts to permeate your soul, but pivot toward the truth instead. Surrender your will and get going.

The environment of pain is where faith can truly flourish. The adversity you experience is inversely proportional to the good that can result from it—not your good, but God's good. This requires having the strength to totally surrender. It means having the drive of a tadpole who reaches the finish line of graduation day, washes the last bit of sand out from behind his ears, and becomes a Navy SEAL.

If your adversity happens to be the death of a loved one whose life was surrendered to Christ, then know you'll see that loved one again. Despite your loss, you can have tremendous hope for the future. Meanwhile, honor that future by living for God today. No matter what the past has inflicted upon you, it's up to you whether you ring out or endure and become stronger.

The enemy begs us to choose the path of least resistance—misery, self-pity, alcohol, drugs, unwise friends, or any such worldly answer will appear to be our easy way out. However, I can guarantee that if you touch that bell, you'll regret it for the rest of your life, knowing what might have been if you had stuck it out to the next evolution. Once you surrender to the trapdoor of sin, the hole only gets deeper and darker until one day the bottom falls out, and you find yourself falling through total darkness.

The only answer is accepting God's everlasting love into your life today and every day, every waking moment. God's Word is your compass board. Jesus is your faithful swim buddy and your only lasting refuge. His love is perfect, and it's the only way to escape the enemy's tricks, illusions, and traps.

Rather than wait for adversity to strike, I've learned to thank God in advance for all things, both good and bad. With this tadpole faith mindset, I face every day with Christ's vision and His bold, fearless attitude. Life is so much more abundant now that I'm free from anxiety, fear, regret, and guilt. Every morning I prepare myself for victory. His purpose dwells in my heart. I thank Him for my present and future storms, not because I'm a Navy frogman but because I belong to Jesus. I'm all His. Every day. Every evolution. Every season. He wins!

Andy Stanley, the pastor of Northpoint Community Church, said he has noticed one thing that's central to all successful marriages: the spouses assume the best about each other no matter the circumstances. Tadpole trust. The same is true in our relationship with God. Without trust, no relationship can work. This trust means complete surrender, boldness, and moving outside our comfort zone.

We've been created for success—not our version of success

but God's. Such success will propel us from self-confidence to God-confidence to true tadpole faith. There's no greater power and no greater reward than living that way.

DARE TO TRUST GOD ALWAYS

- Rather than seek to avoid pain and make your life as comfortable as possible, purposely put yourself in the way of adversity, and use that energy to grow and bless others.

- It's natural to want to avoid pain and seek pleasure, but growth happens largely in the midst of struggle.

- Every morning, be prepared for victory no matter how dire the circumstances. Not because it's easy, but because it's what God commands.

- Remember: Adversity introduces a person to himself . . and to God.

TADPOLE FAITH SUMMATION

GOOD CHOICES LEAD TO GOOD circumstances, and bad choices lead to negative outcomes. We choose, but only the creator of the universe gets to choose what is good . . not the world, you, or me. The sooner we grasp this fact, the more joy and peace we will have, and the happier our lives will be.

The movie *War Room* tells the story of an elderly woman who sets aside a closet space as her "ground zero" for prayer. Rather than fighting with the world's sticks and stones, she pours all her attention into the Psalms and supplications of personal prayer to God. Full of regret for her own prayerless marriage, this woman commits to sharing her "war room" strategy with others. As with any movie, so-called intellectuals and pundits can pick *War Room* apart if they choose. As for me, I walked away from that movie renewed. I'd seen a child of God help others find life through the power of prayer, and she made it look as easy as painting by numbers.

But things aren't always so simple. Today I'm in the midst of a struggle far greater than the cancer that's ravaging my body. My fight is not with free radicals, IRS auditors, or Hell Week instructors, but with "the cosmic powers over this present darkness, against the spiritual forces of evil in the heavenly places" (Ephesians 6:12, ESV). My two oldest sons, although they accepted Christ at an early age, have wandered from their first love. One dismisses prayer as pious mumbling. The other is living on a razor's edge. As a Christian parent, I feel as though my world has turned upside down. Spiritual daggers strike by day, physical pain by night. Rest, for me, no longer exists.

What's a father to do?

In past struggles, the enemy has fought to have me, but by God's beautiful grace, my soul stayed intact, and my life remained in His hands. But now that same enemy has lied his way into the lives of my children, and no matter how many dollars I find in my bank account or how many pounds I press in the gym, there's nothing I can do for them.

How do I fight this new battle? How do I press on to victory? As I watched *War Room*, the answer became abundantly clear: *I don't.*

In 2 Chronicles 20 we find a terrified king named Jehoshaphat who's paralyzed in the face of an impending attack by a horde of warriors from multiple foreign armies. In what seems like a last-ditch effort to avoid utter annihilation, he commits the situation to God, begging the Lord for guidance. He doesn't just pray; he prays with supplication and proclaims a fast throughout Judah. Together Jehoshaphat and the people assemble before the temple and acknowledge their helplessness and seek the help of the only one who can truly save them from their enemies.

Many of us find ourselves in a similar state of helplessness. Husbands, wives, brothers, sisters, children—the people we love most—are tottering on the edge of a spiritual cliff. As we consider this, our souls can be permeated by fear. Like Paul, we wish we could be damned, so that our loved ones could be saved (Romans 9:3). Satan seeks his final stronghold in the earnest desire we feel for the salvation of others.

How will we pray in such circumstances? What does it look like for us to follow the example of Jehoshaphat and the people of Judah?

Well, we could put down our iPhones and head into our own war room to do battle on behalf of others. We could switch off the TV, cut ourselves off from the news and politics of the day, and devote our attention to earnest prayer. We could choose not to eat and invite the pangs of hunger to remind us that God is the one on whom we ultimately rely for everything we have.

The Lord answered Jehoshaphat's prayer in the same way He answers ours: "Do not be afraid! Don't be discouraged by this mighty army, for the battle is not yours, but God's" (2 Chronicles 20:15, NLT). That should have been enough, but God went on to make Himself abundantly clear, commanding the people to meet the advancing enemy head-on: "You will not even need to fight. Take your positions, then stand still and watch the Lord's victory. He is with you. . . . Do not be afraid or discouraged. Go out against them tomorrow, for the Lord is with you!" (2 Chronicles 20:17, NLT). I have to wonder how much sleep Jehoshaphat and his people got that night.

The next morning, not only did they walk out to battle but the king appointed singers to walk ahead of the army, proclaiming praises to the Lord. At that very moment, the Lord caused the opposing armies to start fighting among themselves. When Jehoshaphat and his army finally arrived, all they could see were their enemies' dead bodies. Not a single enemy warrior survived. Just as God had promised, no Israelite had to do so much as lift a finger to experience God's victory.

So how will you pray? Will you hand God a laundry list?

Many of us desperately need a miracle for someone we dearly love. What will you do?

Remember, our battle is not against flesh and blood; it's not against the loved ones who forsake us or the enemies who berate us. This fight doesn't take place on any earthly field of battle. No, our fight is with enemies from the unseen world. We don't battle against people but against the demonic forces that are at war within them. As Paul says: "For we do not wrestle against flesh and blood, but against the rulers, against the authorities, against the cosmic powers over this present darkness, against the spiritual forces of evil in the heavenly places" (Ephesians 6:12, ESV).

Many of us tend to get weirded out when someone brings up spooky things like demons and the devil. For that reason, some churches shy away from using such biblical vocabulary. What they don't realize is that the enemy is prowling about like a lion, seeking people to devour (1 Peter 5:8). It's not as though Satan shows up at our front door with a name badge. Our enemy disguises himself as an angel of light (2 Corinthians 11:14), and his primary goal is to use the people we love to lead us away from God.

We may not have the power to overcome Satan in our own strength, but that doesn't mean we're powerless. God has given us the Holy Spirit, and He has called us to "put on the whole armor of God, that you may be able to stand against the schemes of the devil" (Ephesians 6:11, ESV). Our heavenly Father wants us to *stand*—not retreat, not sit—in the power of His Spirit.

Theologian, preacher, and author J. Vernon McGee once described Satan's "night out" as a Saturday night bender on skid row where bars and drunkenness dominate the scene. Later on, however, McGee came to believe that Satan actually spends his Saturday nights in bed, resting up for church the next morning. Why waste his energy on drunks and outcasts who are already in the bag? Better to put his efforts into winning the souls of those who consider themselves good church people. Lulled into low-profile complacency, these folks line the pews without even the slightest sense of the intense spiritual battle raging all around them. As a result of this complacency, McGee says, "The Word of God sinks in insignificance."[28]

It's so easy to get caught up in our circumstances. We turn on the news and see how nothing seems to make sense anymore. We ask where the good is when all we see is lies, deceit, and hate. We get distracted by focus on the mess and lose sight of the true nature of our spiritual struggle. We forget that God has already told us the nature of the world in His Word. We're just not listening.

It's high time for us to stop, read, and remember what's really going on around us. We have to enter the fight not with the weapons of human strength or psychological might, but with the spiritual weapons of worship, witnessing, and prayer.

In short, we need more war rooms. We need to step into the closet and make it ground zero for our fiercest battles.

It's time we stop going it alone and start getting personal with Jesus. This might be hard, but it's our only path to victory.

SEAL: TADPOLE DAILY HABITS FOR LASTING FAITH

DURING MY LIFE'S STORMS, WITHOUT knowing it at the time, I embraced four important steps that gave me a surpassing vision to see God's purpose for me. No matter how dire life became, I embraced a higher purpose not seen here on earth during my pain. The great news is that it works not only when we're walking into a blazing furnace but whenever we desire earthshaking success. To be fully engaged for such success, the following keys are absolutely necessary to finish the race and win the ultimate prize. Tattoo these SEAL habits onto your heart.

1. **S**cripture

   Everything begins with truth, the creator's spoken Word pinpointed to you. Wisdom always trumps failure, deceit, distractions, and the world's empty promises that lead only to doom. All wisdom begins with God's Word and His promises to you. Pick up the Scriptures and embrace God's Word with enthusiasm. See the Bible for what it is—God's encouragement and directions for you.

2. **E**nvision

   Envision God with you. During my business trials, I placed an extra chair next to mine in my office, so I could envision

Christ beside me and be reminded throughout the day that I was never alone. Envision being God's masterpiece. Envision running the race with confidence. Envision God's promises. Envision being totally focused and locked in, fulfilling His purpose in your life. Envision victory. This is easy when I am constantly reminded of God's presence and respond in praise and prayer.

3. Act

Never in the history of BUD/S training has a tadpole graduated BUD/S and then wanted to immediately retire. Every graduate wants to fulfill the purpose of his training. In the same way, Jesus didn't just talk about His faith; He lived it. He healed the sick. He turned 5 loaves of bread into a feast for 5,000 people. He walked on water to prove a point. He constantly acted with courage in all that He did and ultimately allowed Himself to die on the cross. We are known by our fruit. Words are powerful, but they are useless without action. The amount you give will determine what you get back. The joy in this life is living beyond yourself.

4. Listen to God

Did you know that the average human speaks at a rate of 100 to 200 words per minute? Yet we can listen at a rate of 400 to 600 words per minute. Better yet, we can actually process or think about up to 3,000 words per minute. We are wired to listen more than we talk and to think about five times faster than we hear. According to Stephen Covey, "Most people do not listen with the intent to understand; they listen with the intent to reply."[29] Pray and listen to God. Ask Him to speak to your heart, to reveal His Word, and to show you His presence and assurance in all that you do. Listen with "fiery furnace" faith and begin believing like the champion you were created to be.

NOTES

---

1. Norman Cousins, AZQuotes.com, Wind and Fly, LTD, 2921, https://www.azquotes.com/quote/1138200, last accessed September 15, 2021.

2. M. Scott Peck M.D., *The Road Less Traveled: A New Psychology of Love, Traditional Values and Spiritual Growth* (New York: Touchstone/Simon & Schuster, 1985), no page number.

3. Dr. Sanjay Gupta, "Purpose in Life Is Good for Your Health," Emotional Health, Everyday Health website, reviewed December 7, 2015, htpps://www.everydayhealth.com/news/purpose-life-good-your-health/.

4. Christine Caine.

5. Alex Malley, *The Naked CEO: The Truth You Need to Build a Big Life* (Queensland, Australia: John Wiley & Sons Australia, 2014), no page number.

6. *Remember the Titans*, directed by Boaz Yakin (2000; Burbank, CA: Walt Disney Pictures/Buena Vista, 2001), DVD.

7. "Science Proves the Healing Power of Prayer," March 13, 2015, Health, Newsmax.com, https://www.newsmax.com/amp/health/headline/prayer-health-faith-medicine/2015/03/31/id/635623/.

8. Dr. Martin Luther King Jr., Quotes, goodreads.com, https://www.goodreads.com/quotes/26963-if-you-can-t-fly-then-run-if-you-can-t-runww.goodreads.com/quotes/26963-if-you-can-t-fly-then-run-if-you-can-t-run, last accessed September 15, 2021.

9. Tony Dungy with Nathan Whitaker, *Quiet Strength: The Principles, Practices, and Priorities of a Winning Life* (Carol Stream, IL: Tyndale House, 2008), no page number.

10. Marcus Luttrell with Patrick Robinson, *Lone Survivor: The Eyewitness Account of Operation Redwing and the Lost Heroes of SEAL Team 10* (New York: Back Bay Books, 2008), Page number 231 ISBN 878-0-316-06760-7.

11. C. S. Lewis, *The Problem of Pain* (London: The Centenary Press, 1940), page number 91, ISBN 978-0-06-065296-8.

12. Dale Carnegie, Quotes, goodreads.com, https://www.goodreads.com/quotes/1140103-inaction-breeds-doubt-and-fear-action-breeds-confidence-and-courage, last accessed September 15, 2021.

13. "The Soft Skills Disconnect," National Soft Skills Association website, February 13, 2015, https://www.nationalsoftskills.org/the-soft-skills-disconnect/.

14. John Maxwell.

15. Margaret Thatcher, Quotes, goodreads.com, https://www.goodreads.com/quotes/57583-being-powerful-is-like-being-a-lady-if-you-have, last accessed September 15, 2021.

16. Various versions of this story and the date of the event exist.

17. Kenneth Hildebrand, "Dream Killers (3)," audio, United Christian Broadcasters website, January 9, 2019, https://www.ucb.co.uk/content/dream-killers-3-0.

18. Robert Orben, Quotes, goodreads.com, https://www.goodreads.com/quotes/225763-there-are-only-two-kinds-of-people-in-this-world, last accessed September 15, 2021.

19. "Facts About Suicide," Suicide Prevention, CDC.gov, Center for Disease Control and Prevention, https://www.cdc.gov/suicide/facts/, last accessed September 12, 2021.

20. Hillsong United, "Oceans (Where Feet May Fail)," written by Matt Crock, Joel Houston, and Salomon Ligthelm, published 2013.

21. Robertson Davies, Quotes, goodreads.com, https://www.

goodreads.com/quotes/292873-extraordinary-people-
survive-under-the-most-terrible-circumstances-and-they,
last accessed September 15, 2021.

22. Dr. Martin Luther King Jr..

23. Penn Jillette, "A Gift of a Bible," video, YouTube,
July 8, 2010, https://www.youtube.com/
watch?v=6md638smQd8&t=47s.

24. Victor E. Frankl, *Man's Search for Meaning* (Boston: Beacon
Press, 2006; originally published in 1959), 30.

25. Rick Warren, *The Purpose Driven Life: What on Earth Am I
Here For?* (Grand Rapids, MI: Zondervan, 2002), 278.

26. Nicky Verd, *Disrupt Yourself or Be Disrupted: Escape
Conformity, Reinvent Your Thinking and Thrive in an Era of
Emerging Technologies and Economic Anxiety* (www.nlsa.ac.za,
2019) 95.

27. Warren, *Purpose-Driven Life*, 248.

28. J. Vernon McGee, *Ephesians*, Thru the Bible Commentary
Series, vol. 47, the Epistles (Nashville: Thomas Nelson,
1995), Ch. 6.

29. Stephen R. Covey, *The Seven Habits of Highly Effective People:
Powerful Lessons in Personal Change*, rev. ed. (New York: Free
Press: 2004), 239.

ACKNOWLEDGMENTS

I FIND IT A STRUGGLE to thank the loving people who helped make this book possible. How can words adequately do them justice, and who do I dare leave out? Nonetheless, here I go. I ask for grace for those whose names are not on this page but are written in my heart.

First, thanks to all my buddies in BUD/S Class 89 and the Coronado gods who, by making my life so horrific, gave me the greatest opportunity in the direst moments to see God work in my life, including in the years and decades to come.

Dozens of beautiful souls pitched in with their invaluable commentaries, including Trent Walters, Thomas Womack, Bob, Kenny, Mr. Stobbe, Angie and Leslie Wilson. Their encouragement, as well as support from Eric and Rita in the early days, gave me the added boost to pursue this book. More than just editors, thanks to Kevin Miller and "Surf Girl" Alice Sullivan for their encouragement and expertise. Thanks especially to Alice for her enduring guidance into the uncharted waters of book publishing. Every mastermind group requires someone like Alice who faithfully serves no matter how deep the Tijuana mudflats. A mighty hooyah to Christina Boys—you're a game-changer.

I'm also in debt to my prayer warriors, who continued to call with their encouragement. This list includes people like Steve Williams, Jeff Miller, Jeff Neuber, Tom Carmody, Troy, Chris, Bill and Jan, David, Jared, Brad and Mary Pugh, Durwood, the Destin

Beach Boys, Coach Murdock, Coach Baker, Bea, Craig and Sandy Griffin, Ricky, Jeannie, Elaine, and Dicky and Angela Clark. So thankful to the wonderful people of Rossville, Georgia, for providing me ongoing support and the perfect hometown. Thanks also to my deeply competitive cancer buddy who beat me once again by winning the race to heaven. I'm eager to hug you again soon, Roger "the Man" Bazzell. Your wisdom never failed me.

My Passion City Church was never more than a prayer or call away whenever I needed them. I'm so thankful for my pastors Louie Giglio, Brad Jones, and Chris Boynton, for their faithfulness when Deb and I needed it most. Thanks also to Zig for teaching me that living a faithful life is rich with purpose, excitement, and even corporate success.

A special shout-out for my swim buddy, Guy Cortise, who would share anything with me, as he proved during Hell Week. How can I forget Scott Rawding, Spicker, and my first team commander, Aubrey Davis? Aubrey and Debra were extraordinarily helpful in the final stages of this book. I also dare not forget Mark Van Dyke, who offered his beautiful island home for my writing pleasure.

A special thank you to Dr. Chris Jernigan for becoming and remaining a starburst of bright, shining light that never fades . . even *today*.

Thanks to my mom, dad, and brother who always believed in me, no matter how dire the circumstances. Their approving smiles never wavered, even when not deserved.

Finally, I could not have written a single word of this book without the full-fledged love and support of my faithful bride of twenty-nine years who has long stood at my side no matter how insane my ideas were or are to become. I'm also thankful for my four amazing, God-chosen sons Arin, Evan, Chris, and Avery, who gave me the original catalyst to pour out my feelings on these pages. This book was originally written as a letter to them.

Without them, my faith would not be as intimate, and my witness would be far less (Romans 8:28).

Without any and all of the above, together and jointly, nothing in this book that is worthy would have been possible.

CPSIA information can be obtained
at www.ICGtesting.com
Printed in the USA
LVHW051937261221
706878LV00003B/11/J